GW00992151

Sir Gawain and the Green Knight

Text by
Boria Sax
(Ph.D., SUNY Buffalo)
Department of English
Mercy College
Dobbs Ferry, NY

Illustrations by
Karen Pica

 Research & Education Association

MAXnotes® for
SIR GAWAIN AND THE GREEN KNIGHT

Printed in the United States of America

Library of Congress Catalog Card Number 96-67429

International Standard Book Number 0-87891-044-1

MAXnotes® is a registered trademark of
Research & Education Association, Piscataway, New Jersey 08854

What MAXnotes® Will Do for You

This book is intended to help you absorb the essential contents and features of *Sir Gawain and the Green Knight* and to help you gain a thorough understanding of the work. The book has been designed to do this more quickly and effectively than any other study guide.

For best results, this **MAXnotes** book should be used as a companion to the actual work, not instead of it. The interaction between the two will greatly benefit you.

To help you in your studies, this book presents the most up-to-date interpretations of every section of the actual work, followed by questions and fully explained answers that will enable you to analyze the material critically. The questions also will help you to test your understanding of the work and will prepare you for discussions and exams.

Meaningful illustrations are included to further enhance your understanding and enjoyment of the literary work. The illustrations are designed to place you into the mood and spirit of the work's settings.

The **MAXnotes** also include summaries, character lists, explanations of plot, and section-by-section analyses. A discussion of the work's historical context and language will help you put this literary piece into the proper perspective of what is taking place.

The use of this study guide will save you the hours of preparation time that would ordinarily be required to arrive at a complete grasp of this work of literature. You will be well prepared for classroom discussions, homework, and exams. The guidelines that are included for writing papers and reports on various topics will prepare you for any added work which may be assigned.

The **MAXnotes** will take your grades "to the max."

Dr. Max Fogiel
Program Director

Contents

Each Verse includes List of Characters, Summary, Analysis, Study Questions and Answers, and Suggested Essay Topics.

SECTION ONE

Introduction

The Language of the Gawain Poet

It can be misleading to speak of the Middle English of the Gawain poet as a "language" in the contemporary sense, since neither written nor oral communication was standardized. There were, of course, conventions. If anything, the grammar of Middle English was more complicated than that of modern English. There was, however, no correct or incorrect usage. Spelling and pronunciation were subject to considerable local and individual variations.

This meant that the language was more personal and probably, in some respects, more vivid than our own. There are similar qualities in dialects and in languages such as Yiddish which still are not fully standardized today. It also meant, however, that verse forms, involving such matters as syllable counts, had to be used with less precision than in modern times.

The Gawain poet is part of a movement known as the "alliterative revival" of the thirteenth century. Together with some of his contemporaries, he departed from the forms adopted from Latin languages which were based on rhyme and meter. Instead, he followed Anglo-Saxon poetic traditions, which used heavily stressed words at irregular intervals and alliteration.

Some scholars dispute that this constituted a "revival," since, they maintain, the Anglo-Saxon tradition was never actually eclipsed. We do not have a sufficient number or range of texts to judge with confidence. But such a revival would certainly be consistent with the way in which poetry has developed throughout history. When their immediate predecessors begin to seem either mannered or overly intimidating, poets often react by turning to models in the more distant past.

A similar "alliterative revival" may be found, for example, in the poems of Gerard Manely Hopkins (1844-1889), who used what he called "sprung meter." This involved, like the Anglo-Saxon poems, strongly stressed words at varied intervals, linked together through repetition of sounds. Here, for example, are some lines from his poem "Spring":

> When weeds, in wheels, shoot long and lovely and lush;
> Thrush's eggs look little low heavens, and thrush
> Through the echoing timber does so rise and wring
> The ear, it strikes like lighnings to hear him sing....

Although Hopkins was a very subtle and knowledgeable poetic theorist, his pronunciation of such lines, like his syntax, was often idiosyncratic. He intended five stresses per line, but readers could legitimately scan these lines in other ways.

The work of Hopkins, however, is a good place to start, for a reader who wishes to get a sense of the rich verbal texture of alliterative verse. When we come to the Middle English of the Gawain poet, we must also deal with differences in grammar and vocabulary.

The Middle English of the Gawain poet is, perhaps, roughly as close to modern English as the Dutch language. It is similar to that of Chaucer, though most readers find it slightly more difficult. With a little practice, it is still possible for the non-specialist to read Sir Gawain and the Green Knight in the original, though slowly and with a dictionary.

Only very enthusiastic or adventurous readers, however, are likely to attempt this. For those who do, the edition of the original text used most frequently is the one edited by J. R. R. Tolkien and E. V. Gordon (New York: Oxford U. Press, 1967). For those who would like to try only a few pages, samples of the original are contained with most translations of *Sir Gawain and the Green Knight* including those of Maria Borroff and Brian Stone. A good introduction to the language, containing excerpts from many works, is *A Book of Middle English* by J. A. Burrow and Thorlac Turville-Petre (London: Blackwell, 1993).

Middle English employed approximately the same range of sounds as our current language, but included some symbols that are not used today. Among those symbols are ß/ß ("thorn") and ∂

("eth"), both of which are usually pronounced approximately like the modern English "th" in "that." At ß/ß times might also be pronounced like the modern English "y" in "yet."

Like the pronunciation, the poetic form of the Gawain poet can only be approximately reconstructed. It consisted of verses, each of which contained an irregular number of unrhymed long lines, followed by a rhymed quatrain of short lines. Scholars generally believe that the long lines were generally divided into two parts, each of which generally contained two strong stresses and a varied number of weak stresses. The first three of these strong stresses would alliterate, while the last would not, so they may be rendered as a-a/a-b.

The opening lines of *Sir Gawain and the Green Knight* might, then, be rendered as follows:

> Sißen ße sege and ße assaut / watz sesed at Troye,
> a a / a b
> ße bor brittened and brent / to brondez and askez
> a a / a b
> ße tulk ßat ße trammes / of tresoun ßer wro t
> a a / a b
> Watz tried for his tricherie, / ße trewest on erthe,
> a a / a b

There are other alternatives, as the first half of line two, for example, could very easily be read as having three strong alliterating stresses.

It is important to remember that the poem was intended more for recitiation than for silent reading. The heavy alliteration is particularly effective in reading narrative verse aloud, since it conveys a sense of vigorous motion and dramatic tension. Though perhaps not as elegant as rhyme and meter, it is very easy to respond to. The appeal is so basic that it can accommodate many variations, and the reader need not worry about too much about correctness.

Historical Background

The study of modern literature consists largely in the collection and interpretation of information about the authors. It is almost impossible, for example, to appreciate Byron without thinking of the author and his mystique. We do not, however, even know who the author of *Sir Gawain and the Green Knight* (known as "the Gawain poet") was.

We may view this as a restriction, but, in fact, it does not have to hinder our appreciation very much. We also know nothing substantial of Homer or Dante yet that does not prevent us from numbering them among the finest poets in history. Looked at from one perspective, our comparative ignorance of them and the Gawain poet could even be an advantage. It means there is more room for the imagination.

We should certainly take advantage of the knowledge that is available. Many people find they can enjoy *Sir Gawain and the Green Knight* with little or no knowledge of the author's times. A more sophisticated appreciation, however, will require some understanding of the historical context. Above all, this will help us to respond to the poem not merely as a delightful fantasy but as part of a great tradition.

Only a single copy of *Sir Gawain and the Green Knight* has been preserved from the Middle Ages. The manuscript also contains three other poems, *Pearl, Patience,* and *Purity.* They are written in the dialect of the northwest Midlands, the area of England known today as Lancaster and Yorkshire. Similarities of language, imagery and theme, together with a high level of artistry, have convinced most scholars that they are the work of a single author. *Pearl* is a lament for the death of the author's daughter, while *Patience* retells the Biblical story of Jonah and the whale. *Purity* is a religious meditation in which the author retells many stories from the Old Testament. All are considered to be among the foremost works of medieval literature. A fifth poem, *St. Erkenwald,* is sometimes attributed to the same writer. He was obviously educated in both religious lore and courtly ways, but virtually all our knowledge of him comes from his works.

The Middle Ages has been alternately praised as a period of romance or simple faith and vilified as a time of superstition and ignorance. Perhaps more than any other period of history, it arouses strong emotions. This is because it is a period of strong contrasts: splendid pageantry and squalor, gaiety and despair, compassion and cruelty, asceticism and extravagant sensuality. All of the popular images contain elements of truth, but none of them is complete.

The ethic of the nobility in the Middle Ages is known as chivalry. This is a set of customs that attempted to reconcile the virtues of a warrior society with Christianity. The ethos of the pagan warriors had emphasized physical courage and loyalty to one's tribe and lord. It placed great stress on fierceness in battle and usually regarded restraining influences including pity with disdain. Christianity, on the other hand, upheld an ideal universal love.

Chivalry retained the martial virtues of the pagan warriors but in the service of other ideals. It continued to place great value upon loyalty and courage, but it scorned blood-lust, egotism and unrestrained sexuality. The Knight, the Christian warrior, was expected to be gentle and refined in his domestic life.

Central to the culture of chivalry was the cult of "courtly love." Prior to the Middle Ages, there were only a few literary accounts of idealized lovers in Western culture. Love between the sexes had been regarded as a highly questionable passion, far less worthy of a hero than love of his companions or his country. This changed abruptly around the start of the eleventh century, as the Provencal poets of Southern France began to celebrate erotic love. This new preoccupation quickly spread to Germany and then to the rest of Europe. It became not only the major theme of lyric poetry but also a foundation of the chivalric epics.

Notions of love varied widely, just as they do today. Often a knight would elect to fight in jousting tournaments or on the battlefield in the name of a lady whose favor he wished to win. He was not supposed to expect either physical intimacy or expensive gifts in return, but he might be given a token of the lady such as a sash or a detachable sleeve from her dress. He would then take this with him into battle, sometimes using it as a banner to decorate his lance.

Often a knight might choose to serve the wife of another man. Since marriages among the aristocracy were largely political, love was usually outside of marriage. As long as the love remained only spiritual, the husband was not very likely to object. In practice, however, this sort of service could easily slide into adultery. In Mallory's *Mort D'Arthur*, the downfall of the celebrated Round Table comes when Lancelot, once the greatest of the knights, has a love affair with Queen Guinevere, the wife of King Arthur.

The chivalric ideal of love depended on a very delicate emotional balance. Courtly love may have been an important civilizing force, but it could easily become an occasion for violence as well. It was surrounded by all sorts of elaborate conventions designed to keep erotic passions under reasonable control.

When the Gawain poet wrote at the end of the fourteenth century, the age of chivalry was nearly at an end. An especially virulent outbreak of bubonic plague in 1347-50 had destroyed about a third of the population of Europe and shaken confidence in traditional ways. New weapons including longbows, cannons and muskets were rendering the traditional warfare, together with most of the knightly traditions, obsolete.

As it receded into the past, the age of chivalry began to seem more attractive. The mythical court of King Arthur and his Knights of the Round Table, especially, became surrounded with growing nostalgia. The chivalric knight evolved into the English gentleman.

Even today, there is a good deal in contemporary culture which goes back to chivalry. The cowboy is a modern version of the knight wandering in search of adventure. Soap operas, with their preoccupation with power and adultery, owe quite a bit to chivalric romances.

Almost all literature centers, in one way or another, around human beings, but it does this in many ways. Literature of the Middle Ages frequently emphasized the relationship between humanity and God. With the Renaissance, emphasis shifted more to relationships among different human beings in society. Then, with the romantic movement of the nineteenth century and the environmental movement of the twentieth century, the emphasis again shifts, this time to the relationship between human beings and the natural world.

The change of emphasis that began in the Renaissance was the result of gradual secularization that accompanied the development of science and industry. The reasons for the subsequent emphasis on nature is related to the same process. As human beings transformed more and more of the earth by cutting down woods, draining swamps and building settlements, they began to feel increasingly nostalgic for the primeval landscapes that were being destroyed.

These are only rough generalizations, and the richest and most interesting works from all eras frequently explore all three relationships, as the hero confronts Divine powers, society and nature. This is certainly the case with *Sir Gawain and the Green Knight*. It contains many vivid descriptions of landscapes scattered throughout the poem. These set the mood of the story, but they are also included for their beauty.

Almost all of them emphasize the seasons. The cycle of the year, celebrated in the liturgical calander, provides a sort of frame for the poem. Human life is compared to the year, which as life stirs beneath the snow, then progresses through stages of maturity to a final end.

The powers of nature are sometimes personified in the persons of the Green Knight, who doubles as Sir Bertilak, and Morgan le Fay, who doubles as Lady Bertilak. The Green Knight is a sort of personification of the woods. He is at first completely Green, including his skin, like vegetation. Later, as Sir Bertilak, he changes color, not unlike leaves in fall. He also possesses the mysterious regenerative powers of nature. Like a tree that has lost a limb or even its crown, he simply lives on untroubled.

As for Morgan le Fay, the Green Knight actually calls her a "goddess." To include such a figure is a sort of pagan revival. It anticipates the Renaissance, which was already old in Italy but was just starting to reach England when *Sir Gawain and the Green Knight* was written. Gawain certainly speaks for some of his contemporaries, when he comes across the Green Knight in a desolate place by a fairy mound and wonders if he is a devil.

Nevertheless, both the Green Knight and Morgan le Fay seem to be at least as devout in their Christianity as Arthur and his court. At their home in Hautdesert Castle, they celebrate Mass. Furthermore, though opinions about them will certainly differ, the two certainly have a sense of fairness, and they are at least reasonably benevolent.

If the Green Knight and Morgan le Fay are ambivalent, that reflects the contradictory attitude of people toward the natural world. The landscapes in *Sir Gawain and the Green Knight* may be very beautiful, but most of them are also harsh. Gawain, in his search for the Green Chapel, must not only suffer attacks by wild beasts but also cold and sleet.

The confrontation of humanity with nature found, for medieval aristocrats, its most vivid and exhilarating expression in the hunt. This was not only a means of training for war but also an important social occasion, where people of the castle were bonded in an exciting common endeavor. Ladies would take part as well as men. Each participant had a clearly defined role and a corresponding share of the game. Then the events of the hunt would provide material for tales told around the fire during long winter evenings. Only animals like boars and deer, known for their speed or fierceness, were considered worthy to be hunted by a Lord.

This could be an exciting confrontation, even if it was an unequal one. The forests, however, were actually no more wild than our own. The Gawain poet, anticipating romantics like Tennyson, loves to evoke the terror of primeval landscapes. One of the best examples is this passage:

> By a mountain next morning he Gawain makes his way
> Into a forest fastness, fearsome and wild;
> Oaks old and huge by the hundred together.
> The hazel and the hawthorn were all intertwined
> With rough raveled moss, that raggedy hung,
> With many birds unblithe upon bare twigs
> That peeked most piteously for pain of the cold.
> (Borroff trans., part II, lines 740-747).

Impressive as this description sounds, it is doubtful whether there were any forests this primeval in Britain when the Gawain poet was writing. If there were, they could certainly not have sheltered any big castles, since people needed vast quantities of wood for everything from building to heating in winter. As, in recent years, the study of nature writing has become more popular, scholars have subjected it to greater scrutiny. They have realized that the idea of primal nature unaffected by human activity has usually been a daydream, even if it was a poetic one. Such natural settings had generally ceased to exist even in prehistoric times. Even the Native Americans, it turns out, changed the landscapes where they lived by such means as deliberately starting enormous fires.

The aristocratic hunting preserves of medieval Europe sometimes must have looked very wild, but this was a carefully cultivated illusion. They were tended by foresters, who wanted them to look dark and dangerous, so that hunters might experience their confrontation with nature more vividly. In a way, they were not totally unlike the theme parks of today.

Already, when the Romans conquered Britain around the end of the first century A. D., there were almost no virgin forests. The woodlands had mostly been cut or burned down by original inhabitants. By the early Middle Ages, a cultivated forest known as the "coppice" had become a center of economic and social activity in traditional village life. This was an area where the trees had been, when comparatively young, cut off just above the height of a tall man. This made many small branches grown out in all directions, so they made a sort of tent or canopy. It provided a sort of pleasant, natural shelter. Farmers would take livestock there to feed the animals on nuts and acorns. Markets were held there. The coppice even provided many thin sticks of wood that could be used as staves. The coppice often looked a bit like a gothic church with branches for buttresses. It may even have been the inspiration for the idea of the Green Chapel in *Sir Gawain and the Green Knight.*

This aspect of traditional British life ended in some areas when William of Normandy conquered Britain in 1066. He desired to greatly expand the royal game preserves. In some cases he went so far as to destroy buildings and even entire villages to make way for the forests. These forests sometimes became a refuge for political dissidents, the most famous of whom is the legendary Robin Hood.

However the British forests were somewhat wild in at least one respect. It was very difficult to map them accurately. Without the benefit of a compass, which did not become widespread until the end of the Middle Ages, it was, additionally, very difficult to find one's way. Knights in search of adventure might ride out into the forest. They could never know in advance whom or what they might find. Gawain sets out into the forest to seek the Green Knight, without a map or direction, trusting only to providence

In summary, the relationship between human beings and the natural world is one of our most urgent concerns in the late twentieth century. Since nature, however, has long been formed by human activity, we can certainly never expect to understand it apart from history. *Sir Gawain and the Green Knight* would be a good book to take with you on a camping trip. You might gaze up from the fire and imagine Hautdesert Castle somewhere among the trees.

The Figure of Sir Gawain

Gawain was probably the earliest of the Arthurian heroes. Scholars associate him closely with the Irish hero Cú Chulaind. An adventure of Cú Chulaind in the tale of *Bricriu's Feast*, which is usually dated to the eighth or ninth century, appears to be an early version of the story of *Sir Gawain and the Green Knight*. Cú Chulaind and two other warriors have each claimed to be the champion at the court. To settle the dispute, a judge sends all three to the sorcerer Utath, who proposes a test. The champion must behead Utath, who will then return the next day and cut off the head of the warrior. Only Cú Chulaind has the courage to accept this challenge. After being decapitated, Utath picks up his head and walks away. He returns the next day with his head back on his shoulders, and, fulfilling the bargain, Cú Chulaind stretches out his neck. Utath brings an ax down of Cú Chulaind's neck three times, but does not hurt him. Instead, the sorcerer tells Cú Chulaind to rise and declares him the champion.

Gawain is mentioned in Geoffrey of Monmoth's *History of the Kings of England* as Arthur's nephew and as the greatest of British warriors. He later retains some of the roughness of his Pagan heritage. In the Arthurian romances of *Cretien de Troyes*, Gawain is associated with magic and unrestrained sexuality. In later Arthurian romances, he is generally overshadowed by figures such as Lancelot, Percival, Galahad and Bors. He often is described as a knight who is the model of secular virtue but for whom the mystical heights are unattainable. In Mallory's *Mort D'Arthur* and other romances, Gawain is given a feature that may go back to a Pagan deity associated with the sun. His strength increases, like that of the sun, in the morning, peaks at noon and then declines.

The portrayals of him vary widely, but one feature is remarkably consistent. Sir Gawain does not appear entirely Christian, at least by comparison with other knights. He belongs to a slightly different world, whether this is one of sorcery, archaic warfare or simply secular concerns.

Perhaps the Gawain poet, in choosing Gawain as his protagonist, was deliberately trying to return to earlier Arthurian traditions. Lancelot and Bors are mentioned in his romance, but they are not given the same prominence as in other tales. Gawain appears to be foremost of Arthur's knights, just as he was at the beginning of the cycle.

One innovation of the Gawain poet was, however, his handling of Gawain's alienation at the court of Arthur. While the others at Camelot seem to view chivalry largely as a matter of pageantry and fine manners, Gawain takes the ethical obligations of his code far more seriously. The exploration of alienation as a poetic theme is a remarkably modern feature in *Sir Gawain and the Green Knight.*

The Figure of the Green Knight

The mysterious Green Knight is the most unique, and perhaps most memorable, feature of *Sir Gawain and the Green Knight.* Scholars have long debated whether he owes more to Pagan mythology, to poetic invention or folkloric ceremony. However that may be, he represents a spirit of vegetation. Trees can live far longer than human beings, and they have regenerative powers that people have always envied. A person who loses a limb is permanently handicapped, but a tree that loses a limb will simply grow in another direction. The Green Knight has this ability. On being decapitated, he simply picks up his head, which continues to speak in his hand. The next year, the head is back on his torso where it belongs.

While he has, as we shall explain later, numerous possible predecessors in literature, the Green Knight is a figure primarily known through the visual arts. The Green Man is a familiar figure in the sculpture of churches, especially from approximately eleventh century on. He would be composed of vegetative forms, often leaves. Sometimes he would grimace at the worshippers. He might also smile or simply stare in front of him. At times, he would be a knight, but he is not consistently identified with any sector of medieval society. It may be that there were legends associated with the Green Man, but he could also have been used primarily for decorative purposes.

Nevertheless, possible literary predecessors of the Green Knight may go back almost to the start of civilization. The earliest is the giant Humbaba, guardian of the cedar forest of Lebanon in the ancient Mesopotamian *Epic of Gilgamesh* from around the early second millennium B. C. Like the Green Man of medieval Europe, Humbaba was often sculpted grimacing from the facades of

buildings. There is also a Muslim Green Man known as Kadr, whose lore was probably carried by crusaders back from the Holy Land. There is only one other popular tale from the European Middle Ages in which the Green Knight plays an important role, the story of the brothers Valentine and Orson at the court King Peppin in France. The Green Knight has captured a princess, and challenged all knights who aspire to rescue her to do battle with him. When he defeats the knights, he hangs them from a tree.

The time comes for Orson, who was raised by a bear, to do battle with the Green Knight. Orson, who has lived as a wild man, at first does not wish to put on armor, but Valentine and his companions insist. After the battle with the Green Knight has begun, Orson notices that any wounds he inflicts on his adversary with lance or sword heal at once. Orson then jumps from his horse, takes off his armor, throws away his weapons, and precedes to battle the Green Knight in his old way, using nothing but a club. Forcing the Green Knight from his horse by sheer strength, Orson is victorious. After being defeated, the Green Knight converts to Christianity and becomes a fairly benevolent figure.

The tale does not enter English literature until the first decade of the sixteenth century with a translation by Henry Watson from the French original published only about a decade before. Scholars, however, believe the tale goes back at least to a lost manuscript in French from the early fourteenth century, perhaps much further. The popular story could certainly have been known to the author of *Sir Gawain and the Green Knight*.

The Green Knight in *Valentine and Orson* seems to be partly of Eastern origin, since he initially worships the god Mohammad. Green is the color of Islam. The way this Green Knight has his adversaries hung from a tree, however, suggests a possible connection with the Pagan god Odin or Woton. Human sacrifices to the Norse deity were made in this manner.

It is also possible that the Green Knight, in the form of the hunter Bertilak, may be a version of the Wild Huntsman of European folklore. This is a figure who leads a hunting party through the sky, and he is usually condemned on account of some crime to hunt for all eternity. The wild huntsman has been variously identified as the Norse god Odin, as King Arthur, as Hearn the Hunter

and many other figures. The author of *Sir Gawain and the Green Knight* may have drawn the character from many sources, but it was poetic imagination that enabled him to produce such a vivid figure.

Whatever his origins, the Green Man, including his incarnation as a knight, remains prominent in popular culture today. He probably influenced tales of the romantic outlaw Robin Hood, whose men were always dressed in green. Sculptures of the Green Man of stone and plaster are increasingly popular as ornaments for the home and garden. A large produce company has adopted the "Green Giant" as its emblem, and sometimes the Green Man has even been used as a symbol of the ecology movement.

Master List of Characters

King Arthur—*The legendary king of Britain, at whose court the story begins. Husband of Guinivere and uncle of Gawain, he presides over the famed Knights of the Round Table at Camelot, which are the subject of numerous romances from the start of the Middle Ages through the present. Some scholars believe he was originally a tribal chieftain in Britain, while others trace him to a solar deity.*

Queen Guinevere—*The wife of Arthur. According to legend, she had an affair with Sir Lancelot which brought about the fall of the Round Table. Her adversary is the enchantress Morgan le Fay, who, we learn at the end of the poem, conjured the Green Knight in order to terrify Guinevere.*

Sir Gawain—*The nephew of Arthur and a knight. He accepts the challenge of the Green Knight, whom he must behead, then seek out next year (see separate section).*

Bishop Baldwin—*Religious figure, who in the beginning of the poem, sits next to King Arthur*

The Duke of Clarence—*Attends the feast in the beginning of the poem.*

Sir Ywain, Sir Eric, Sir Dodinal le Sauvage, Sir Bors, Sir Bedivere, Sir Lionel, Sir Lucan the Good and Sir Mador de la Porte—*Knights of the Round Table.*

Sir Agravain á la dure main—*A knight; Gawain's brother.*

Sir Lancelot—*A knight; has an affair with Queen Guinevere.*

The Green Knight—*The mysterious man in Green whom Gawain, in response to a challenge, beheads and must later seek at the Green Chapel.*

Gringolet—*The horse of Gawain.*

Peter—*Porter who welcomes Gawain to Hautdesert Castle.*

Lord Bertilak—*Lord of the castle of Hautdesert, where Gawain stays on his way to find the Green Knight. At the end of the story, he is revealed to be the Green Knight himself.*

Lady Bertilak—*Wife of Lord Bertilak, who tries to seduce Gawain three times while her husband is away. When Gawain refuses her advances, she gives him a sash, which she says has the magical property of preserving him from harm from weapons. When Gawain first sees Lady Bertilak, she is accompanied by and old crone, Morgan le Fay, and some scholars maintain they are different incarnations of a single person.*

Old Crone / Morgan le Fay—*The woman first who accompanies Lady Bertilak when Gawain first arrives at castle Hauptdesert. She appears ugly as her younger companion is beautiful. The Green Knight later tells Gawain that he had been conjured by Morgan le Fay to frighten her adversary queen Guinevere. Morgan is closely associated with Lady Bertilak, and some scholars think they are the same. In Arthurian romances in general, Morgan is a powerful and ambivalent sorceress, who often lays temptations for the knights of King Arthur. Scholars believe she was orginally a goddess of the sea.*

Gawain's Guide—*A servant who accompanies Gawain from castle Hauptdesert to the Green Knight. He tells Gawain how ruthless the Green Knight is, then he turns back in fear.*

Summary of the Poem

The stories begins amid the festivities of New Year's Eve at the court of King Arthur. A great feast is being prepared, but King Arthur has vowed not to eat until he has heard strange news or a challenge has been issued at his court. His desire is quickly fulfilled, as a huge Green Knight appears in the door, holding a holly branch in one hand and a battle–ax in the other. All stare at the stranger in fear, but he explains that he has come in peace.

He proceeds, however, to taunt the knights, and issues a challenge. Any knight may take the ax, and chop off the head of the Green Knight. After doing so, however, that knight must seek out the Green Knight at the same time next year, at which time the Green Knight will behead his adversary. At first, nobody will accept the challenge. Then, fearing that his entire court will be shamed, Arthur himself takes it up. At this point, Gawain volunteers.

Gawain chops off the head of the Green Knight, who then retrieves his head, carries it to his horse and mounts. The Green Knight holds up his head in his hand in front of Gawain. The severed head reminds Gawain of his promise, then it directs Gawain to seek him in the Green Chapel.

The next year on the first of November Gawain sets out to find the Green Chapel. After surviving many perils, he comes to a beautiful castle in the deep wood. He is welcomed by Bertilak (not named until later), Lord of the castle. There are many knights and ladies, but Gawain notices especially a beautiful woman, the wife of Bertilak, beside an old crone.

The next morning, Bertilak is about to go hunting, and he makes an agreement with Gawain. He will bring Gawain whatever game he kills, but Gawain must give Bertilak whatever he might receive during the day. The wife of Bertilak comes to talk with Gawain, and gives him a kiss as she departs. Bertilak brings Gawain a stag he has killed, and Gawain gives Bertilak a kiss.

On the second day, Bertilak goes hunting once again. Lady Bertilak visits Gawain, and this time she is more aggressively seductive. Gawain refuses her advances. On leaving, she gives Gawain two kisses. Bertilak returns and gives Gawain an enormous boar. Gawain, in return, gives Bertilak two kisses.

Bertilak also goes hunting on the third day. Lady Bertilak once more tries to seduce Gawain but is again unsuccessful. She then offers Gawain a precious ring, but he will not take it. Finally, she offers him her sash, saying it is far less precious than the ring but has magical properties. It can, she maintains, make the wearer invulnerable to any weapon. Hoping to save himself from the Green Knight through magic, Gawain accepts. As she leaves, Lady Bertilak gives Gawain three kisses. Bertilak returns, and brings Gawain a fox. Gawain gives Bertilak the three kisses, but he says nothing about the sash.

The next morning, accompanied by a guide, Gawain sets out to find the Green Knight. His servant becomes very frightened and decides to leave. Gawain hears the sharpening of an ax. Then the Green Knight appears. Gawain bends his neck, and the Green Knight raises the ax. As the Green Knight lowers the ax, Gawain flinches. The Green Knight checks his blow and complains. Gawain lowers his neck a second time. The Green Knight raises his ax then lowers it, but checks the blow once more. This time he praises Gawain for not flinching. Gawain complains angrily, and demands that the Green Knight finish the job. Once again, Gawain bows his head and the Green Knight raises the ax. This time he nicks the neck of Gawain, but he does not decapitate him.

No longer bound by the agreement, Gawain prepares to defend himself. The Green Knight, however, explains that he was Sir Bertilak, and he and his wife were conjured by the sorceress Morgan le Fay, the old crone at his castle. The two checked blows, the Green Knight explains, were for the honorable behavior shown by Gawain, in refusing to be seduced by Lady Bertilak. The nick was for dishonorably taking the sash.

Gawain wishes to return the sash, but Bertilak insists that he keep it. Gawain says that he will wear it as a token of his shame. When he returns home, however, Arthur and the knights and ladies, are delighted by the story. They follow his example and wear green baldrics, not in shame but in honor of Gawain.

Estimated Reading Time

There are several good translations of *Sir Gawain and the Green Knight* available, but that of Marie Borroff (New York: Norton, 1967) is the overwhelming favorite of scholars. Not only does it do an excellent job of recreating the formal qualities of the original but it is also very lucid and easy to read. More widely available, however, and almost as finely wrought, is the translation by Brian Stone (New York: Penguin, 1988). The translation by Borroff numbers the lines, while that of Stone numbers the verses. I have indicated both in the commentary, so the reader using either translation will be able to use this book without difficulty.

The poem comprises a bit more than two thousand five hundred lines. An initial reading of a translation should take about two and a half hours. The reader should make a minimum of interruptions and go at a relaxed but steady pace. This way the rhythmic flow of the poem will not be broken. With such a complex, sophisticated and thoughtful work, the reader can never expect, however, to appreciate everything in a single reading. He or she will probably wish to go back over some details and perhaps to read the entire work more than once. Many people have devoted their entire lives to this work, and nobody will ever understand it completely. Every reader needs, at a certain point, to decide how much understanding is enough.

Part One

Verses 1-10 (Lines 1-231)

New Characters:

King Arthur: *the legendary king at Camelot, who is presiding over Christmas festivities*

Queen Guinevere: *the wife of King Arthur, famed for her beauty*

Sir Gawain: *the nephew of King Arthur and hero of the story*

The Green Knight: *the mysterious stranger; a huge man whose clothes and complexion are green; he arrives in Camelot at the Christmas festivities to deliver the strange challenge which begins the story*

Bishop Baldwin: *religious figure, who in the beginning of the poem, sits next to King Arthur*

The Duke of Clarence: *attends the feast in the beginning of the poem*

Sir Ywain, Sir Eric, Sir Dodinal le Sauvage, Sir Bors, Sir Bedivere, Sir Lionel, Sir Lucan the Good and Sir Mador de la Porte: *knights of the Round Table*

Sir Agravain á la dure main: *a knight; Gawain's brother*

Sir Lancelot: *a knight; has an affair with Queen Guinevere*

Summary

The poet leads into his story by telling of the foundation of Britain and the line of King Arthur. The story begins as Arthur and his court are celebrating the Christmas holidays. There are contests and games. People attend Mass and exchange gifts. A feast is being prepared and Queen Guinevere sits in a place of honor on a dais under a costly canopy with silk curtains and imported tapestries. On her left is seated Sir Gawain, and next to him is his brother Sir Agravain. The seat on her right waits for Arthur. The restless young king has vowed not to feast until either he has heard a tale of some wonder or else a challenge has been issued to one of the knights of the Round Table.

Suddenly a stranger, the Green Knight, appears in the doorway. He is at least a head taller than any of Arthur's knights. He is also very well-proportioned, but his complexion and his clothing are green, with a few touches of gold. Even his hair and beard are green. His horse, similarly splendid, is entirely green as well.

The knights think what a formidable adversary the Green Knight must be, yet he wears no armor. He holds a strand of holly in one hand and an enormous battle-ax in the other. The Green Knight calls for the whomever is presiding over the feast.

Analysis

According to tradition, the crown of Arthur went all the way back to King Priam of Troy. The third stanza alludes to several stories connected with this origin. The Greeks had burned the city, but Aeneas, son of Priam, escaped, and his descendants had founded many kingdoms including Rome and Tuscany. Felix Brutus, a great grandson of Aeneas, had founded Britain and started the dynasty of Arthur. The kingdom, the poet says, had seen many wonders, but the greatest of all may be the tale he is about to recount.

Though the opening may initially seem like the proud invocation of illustrious ancestors, it is actually more complex. By tracing the rise of Britain and the court of Arthur to the burning of Troy, the author is reminding us that earthly splendor does not last forever. Furthermore, he also reminds us that the rulers of mighty nations are fallible human beings, who may be destroyed by greed or pride. Aeneas, for example, was, according to some traditions, guilty of treacherously conspiring with his companion Antenor against the city of Troy.

Nations usually mythologize their origins, yet the myths of national origins often contain some crime by the founders which must be expiated. The ancient Greeks, for example, traced their origin to the Homeric heroes, yet they often felt these founders of the Greek nation showed both cruelty and dishonesty in their capture of Troy. The Hebrews traced their origin to the kingdom of David and Solomon, yet both these rulers sometimes behaved in ways that were less than worthy. In a similar way, the British, like the Romans, traced their origins to Aeneas, who was sometimes condemned for treason.

In America, we often take a similarly ambivalent view of our founding fathers such as Thomas Jefferson, who proclaimed noble principles but kept slaves. King Arthur and his court were viewed as ancestral figures by many peoples, not only in Britain but in the rest of Europe. In the *Sir Gawain and the Green Knight*, we can see both their glory and their failings.

By invoking these mythic ancestors, the author establishes a mood of gravity. It is a bit like an American public official invoking George Washington at the beginning of a speech, in order to set a dignified tone. The Gawain poet, however, is exalting Arthur and his knights in order to deflate them, or at least show them as human and fallible, in the scene that is to come. The portraits of Arthur and his knights are nearly always affectionate but often satirical.

There is some subtle criticism in the description of Queen Guinevere. She is set apart from the guests on a dais, surrounded by too much luxury. More significantly, she is glancing around flirtatiously, and all of the knights are overwhelmed by her beauty.

Arthur is young and restless. His vow not to eat until he has either heard a wondrous tale or a challenge has been issued seems to invite trouble. It is an indication that he has become bored. In spite of all the merriment, all is not well at the court.

The descriptions all emphasize the magnificence of the court, but they say nothing about the character of Arthur and his knights. In the Middle Ages, just as today, people had an ambivalent attitude toward displays of wealth. Christian moralists often condemned them as vanity, yet even the church constantly displayed jewels and

precious metals. The poet seems to simultaneously admire the wealth and view it as a source of danger.

The Green Knight is so strange and so physically intimidating that, on arriving, he immediately dominates the scene. The holly branch in one hand, a plant that remains green throughout the year, is a symbol of life. The ax in the other hand, an implement used largely for executions, is a symbol of death. These cosmic symbols suggest he has a mission of enormous significance. That he should call for the person directing the festivities is a rebuke to Arthur for not providing serious leadership.

Study Questions

1. Who according to tradition, founded the dynasty of Arthur?

2. Where was the court of Arthur?

3. At what time of year does the story begin?

4. Why is Arthur not yet seated?

5. Next to whom is Gawain seated?

6. Next to whom, apart from Guinevere, is the seat of Arthur?

7. How tall is the Green Knight?

8. Is the Green Knight equipped to do battle?

9. What has the Green Knight in his hands?

10. For whom does the Green Knight call?

Answers

1. According to tradition, the dynasty of Arthur was founded by Felix Brutus, great grandson of the Trojan hero Aeneas.

2. The court of Arthur was at Camelot.

3. The story begins at Christmas Eve.

4. Arthur has sworn not to eat until he has either heard a marvel or a challenge has been issued.

5. Gawain is seated beside Guinevere and by his brother Agravain.

6. Arthur is seated between Guinevere and Bishop Baldwin.

7. The Green Knight is almost a giant, far taller than any of Arthur's knights.

8. No, the Green Knight is not wearing armor.

9. In one hand the Green Knight holds a branch of holly, in the other a battle-ax.

10. The Green Knight calls for whomever is presiding at the gathering.

Suggested Essay Topics

1. Compare and contrast the Christmas celebrations at the court of Arthur with a contemporary Christmas.

2. According to some scholars, the poem may have been inspired by English folk plays for the Christmas season. In that case, the role of the Green Knight might have been analogous to that of Saint Nicholas, Father Christmas or, in contemporary times, Santa Claus. Compare the Green Knight to one or more of these figures that personify Christmas.

3. Admirers of President John F. Kennedy sometimes referred to his administration as "Camelot" after the legendary court of King Arthur. His detractors sometimes used the same name, but in an ironic way. What do you think was the reason for this designation? Was it appropriate? Why or why not?

4. Compare the court at Camelot with other mythologized portraits of ancestors, such as, for example, the Homeric heroes or the founding fathers of America.

Verses 11-21 (Lines 232-490)

Summary

All stare at the Green Knight in amazement. Finally, Arthur courteously introduces himself, and he invites the stranger to stay with them. The Green Knight explains that he does not intend to stay, yet he has come in peace. Arthur tells the Green Knight that, if he has come for combat, the knights of the Round Table will oblige him. The Green Knight taunts the knights of the Round Table, saying that they are just boys and would certainly not have been able to stand up to him in battle if that was his mission.

The Green Knight goes on to offer a challenge. Any knight may take up the ax he has brought and cut off his head. That knight, however, must seek him out at his home at the same time next year, and let the Green Knight behead the challenger.

Nobody rises to accept the challenge, so the Green Knight taunts the men as cowards and begins to laugh. This goads Arthur himself into accepting the challenge. He picks up the ax and is about to behead the Green Knight. Then Gawain calls out and volunteers to take the challenge on himself in Arthur's place.

The king agrees, and tells Gawain to make the first blow count, so the Green Knight will not be able to retaliate. The Green Knight expresses his satisfaction. Gawain asks the Green Knight where he lives, and the Green Knight says he will tell that after Gawain has fulfilled the first part of their agreement. He bows his neck a bit. Gawain raises the ax and cuts off the head of the Green Knight. People turn aside as it rolls around the floor. The Green Knight, however, goes after his head, retrieves it and carries it to his horse.

After he has mounted, the Green Knight lifts his head with his arm. The severed head addresses Gawain. It reminds Gawain to fulfill his part of the bargain. Gawain must seek him at the Green Chapel. Many people know him as "the Knight of the Green Chapel," the head explains, and they will be able to show the way.

As soon as the Green Knight has left, Arthur tells Guinevere not to be dismayed, adding that such events are appropriate to the Christmas season. He calmly directs Gawain to hang up the ax and gives orders for the feast to continue.

Analysis

This passage is full of humor, as the challenge of the Green Knight reveals the weaknesses of Arthur's court. Arthur is eager to see combat. The knights are willing to risk their lives in dangerous jousting tournaments, for no other purpose than entertainment. They are, however, at a loss to respond to the challenge of the Green Knight.

There is no clear reason why anybody should accept the strange proposal of the Green Knight, but, as young men, Arthur

and his knights are unable to resist a dare. The taunt about the knights being just boys clearly infuriates Arthur, but that response suggests that it is at least partially true. The knights of the Round Table have the reckless courage of youth, but they lack a mature appreciation of mortality.

The Green Knight is a spirit of vegetation, which dies and is reborn every year. He asks the people at Camelot to accept death not simply as a danger, which adds to the thrill of combat, but as the inevitable end of life. To chop off his neck is to accept the passing of the year, and with it some of the youth and glory of Camelot. To seek out the chapel of the Green Knight, so that the bargain can be fulfilled, is to accept the inevitability of death. The year, as in much medieval lore, is made to stand for the span of a human life.

The challenge, in other words, is to progress from reckless daring, which is based on the illusion that one cannot die, to mature courage. It is a sort of transition that, even today, must be made, for example, by young recruits into the military who have been given glamorized accounts of war. In fact, this is a universal part of human experience, that all men and women must confront as they grow older. In this respect, heroes like the knights of the Round Table are no different from other people.

Arthur initially accepts the challenge, though he seems to do it solely out of pride. When Gawain volunteers, it is for a reason that may seem less romantic but, at least from a pragmatic point of view, is more substantial. The young knight is trying to save Arthur. Even at the start, he is showing greater maturity than his king.

But, even in this, there is a slight hint of ambivalence. Gawain is sitting next to Guinevere, and perhaps he is acting partially to impress her. Like Lancelot, Gawain has been romantically linked with Guinevere in other writings. By volunteering here, he is stepping into the place of Arthur, which might help explain why the king later does not seem particularly grateful afterwards.

The Green Knight is so imposing that Gawain realizes the bargain is dangerous, even though the blow to his adversary would normally be fatal. Though Arthur tells Gawain that if the initial stroke is successful, retaliation will be unlikely, it is hard to know to what extent the king really believes this. At any rate, there is a humorous contrast between the calm man about to be beheaded and the tense executioners.

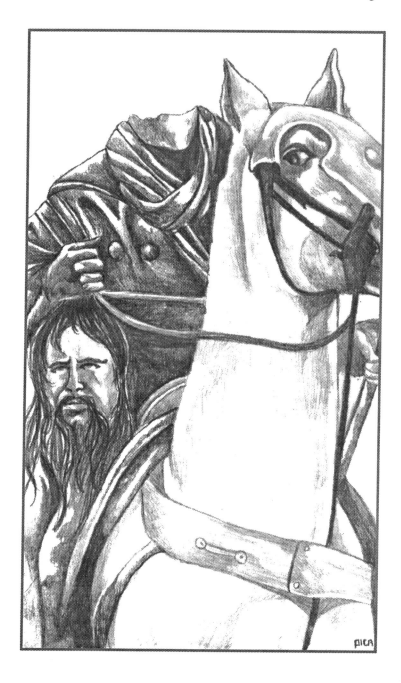

When Gawain, before striking the blow, asks the Green Knight where he lives, the young knight, once again, shows greater honor and maturity than his king. The question shows, first of all, that Gawain is not by any means confident that the Green Knight will not survive the blow. Furthermore, it shows that he is serious about fulfilling his part of the bargain.

The Green Knight, addressing his final words to Gawain, says he is known to many as the "Knight of the Green Chapel." This suggests that he is a figure of widespread folkloric traditions. Perhaps King Arthur and his knights do not know of him simply because they are isolated from other people by the splendor of the court.

The phrase "Green Chapel" may refer to a particular location, but the geography of folklore tends to be rather flexible. The vaults of Gothic chapels resembled trees whose tops converge in the forest canopy. The Green Knight could also be saying that he is always present in the woods.

After the Green Knight has left, the initial response of Arthur is to address words of comfort to Guinevere. His treatment of Gawain seems ungrateful and even a bit callous, when he directs the ax to be hung up and the feasting to begin. As a king, he cannot be as open about his feelings as other people, and it is hard to know how much he really appreciates what Gawain has done.

When he says that the strange episode is appropriate to the season, the effect is partly humorous. The Christmas season was largely a time of gaiety, and festivities often involved good- natured pranks and jokes. The remark of Arthur could also indicate an inability to appreciate or comprehend danger.

Study Questions

1. What is Arthur's initial offer to the Green Knight?

2. Is the Green Knight wearing armor? Is he carrying a weapon?

3. How does the Green Knight taunt the Knights of the Round Table?

4. According to the bargain proposed by the Green Knight, what may an adversary who accepts his challenge do to him?

5. What must the adversary later do to complete the bargain?

6. What is the initial response of the knights of the Round Table to the challenge of the Green Knight.

7. Who first accepts the challenge?

8. Who finally beheads the Green Knight?

9. What does the Green Knight do on being beheaded?

10. By what name does the Green Knight say he is commonly known?

Answers

1. Arthur offers the Green Knight hospitality, and says the stranger may give his reason for coming at the appropriate time.

2. No, the Green Knight is not wearing armor and carries no weapon but the ax.

3. The Green Knight calls the knights of the Round Table "boys," and states that they are too young to match him in combat.

4. An adversary may behead the Green Knight.

5. The adversary must then find the Green Knight and allow himself to be beheaded.

6. The knights of the Round Table initially sit in silence on hearing the challenge.

7. King Arthur initially accepts the challenge.

8. Sir Gawain finally beheads the Green Knight.

9. On being beheaded, the Green Knight retrieves his head, then carries it to his horse and mounts.

10. The Green Knight says he is commonly known as the "Knight of the Green Chapel."

Suggested Essay Topics

1. Was Arthur right or wrong to accept the challenge of the Green Knight? If he was wrong, what do you think he should have done?

2. Why does the Green Knight wait until his head has already
    been chopped off to say how he can be found?

3. After the Green Knight has left, Arthur acts calm, but what
    do you think he is really thinking?

4. Retell the first part of *Sir Gawain and the Green Knight* in
    the first person, adopting the point of view of a character
    such as Gawain, Guinevere or Gawain's brother, Agravain.
    Perhaps the various characters may perceive events in very
    different ways.

Part Two

Verses 22-34 (Lines 491-810)

New Characters:

Gringolet: *Gawain's horse*

Peter: *the porter who welcomes Gawain to Hautdesert Castle*

Summary

The year passes quickly. Gawain celebrates at the court of Arthur on November 1, All Saints' Day. On the following day, All Souls' Day, he takes leave of his companions and sets out on his horse Gringolet to find the Green Knight.

Gawain wears splendid armor, and his shield is adorned with the symbol of the pentangle painted in red gold on the outside and a picture of the Virgin Mary on the inside. The narrator describes the symbolic meaning of the pentangle, which he said was conceived by Solomon. It is called by the English, he says, "the endless knot," since it may be drawn with a single line. It has five points, a mystic number.

Nobody Gawain meets knows the way to the Green Chapel. The journey proves perilous, and he must battle many adversaries: dragons, wolves, wild men, bulls, bears, boars and ogres. The land is cold and inhospitable.

Finally Gawain passes through a grove of ancient trees, and glimpses a beautiful castle in the distance. It is surrounded by a double moat, above which rise many towers and turrets. As Gawain approaches, a porter comes to greet him.

Analysis

Gawain sets out on All Souls' Day, which is a Christian holiday set close to the time of the Celtic celebration of Sauin, when the border between the world of human beings and that of spirits, according to tradition, would disappear. The Christian overlay never entirely replaced the original meaning of the period, and many celebrations associated with it are similar to those of Halloween. Both All Souls' Day and Halloween, for example, often involves the lighting of candles and even contacting the dead.

The story of the *Sir Gawain and the Green Knight* fuses many traditions, and the author was doubtless aware that the time had both religious and popular significance. While Gawain undertakes his journey out of high ethical standards appropriate to a Christian knight, the journey involves him in a world of archaic magic. It is a quest that his companions at the Round Table fail to understand.

The author must have attached great importance to the description of the pentangle on Gawain's shield, since it is the only time in the poem that he departs from the role of narrator to speak in philosophical terms. The symbol goes back to the earliest civilizations of the Near East. The primary use of the symbol has been in alchemy and the occult, though it sometimes appears in ecclesiastical materials as well. It later came to be regarded as a Satanic symbol, which is the way many people think of it today, though the Gawain poet certainly had nothing of the sort in mind.

Medieval lore often centered on mystic numbers. The poet tells us at great length how the number five, corresponding to the points of the pentangle, is the number of the senses (wits), joys and virtues. It is difficult to reduce the meaning of this symbol, as used in the poem, to a single word or phrase. Perhaps, however, it may be summarized as wholeness and purity.

Although the population of Europe in the Middle Ages was relatively thin, at least by modern standards, old forests were very rare. There were no synthetic materials, and nearly everything that was not cloth, stone or metal had to be made out of wood. Large quantities of wood were needed, for example, for furniture, staves, ships and, above all, heating during winter. Furthermore, woods were used as a place for pasturing swine, as well as for socializing.

A large castle, therefore, would not actually be surrounded by

many ancient trees, as Hautdesert Castle is in the poem. Such a castle in the depths of a virgin forest, however, is a conventional motif in medieval romances, and it is also found in popular fairy tales such as those of the *Brothers Grimm*. The untouched trees are a sign that the castle could only appear through magic.

The Gawain poet is noted for his descriptive powers, and this section contains some of the most notable examples. Especially vivid, for example, is the description of the passing year at the start (verses 22 & 23) and the description of the castle in the woods (verses 32-34). Those interested in poetic technique may wish to pay special attention to them.

Study Questions

1. When does Gawain leave Camelot to seek the Green Knight?
2. How do the lords and ladies respond to Gawain's departure?
3. What is the last thing Gawain does before his departure?
4. What does Gawain have painted on the outside of his shield?
5. What is the design of a pentangle?
6. What does Gawain have on the inside of his shield?
7. What are the five virtues connected with the five points of the pentangle?
8. Is the journey of Gawain difficult?
9. What does Gawain do when he comes to the deep woods?
10. Who first greets Gawain when he comes to Haudesert castle?

Answers

1. He leaves on All Souls' Day.
2. They grieve for him, since he may not return.
3. The last thing Gawain does before his departure is to hear Mass.
4. Gawain has a pentangle painted on the outside of his shield.
5. A pentangle is a five-pointed star, drawn in a single line without a beginning or end.

6. Gawain has a picture of the Virgin Mary etched on the inside of his shield.

7. The five virtues are generosity, kindness, continence, courtesy and piety.

8. Yes, the journey is extremely difficult. Gawain has to contend with adversaries such as dragons and wild men, as well as with loneliness and cold.

9. When he comes to the deep woods, Gawain prays to Mary for a place to hear mass.

10. A servant first greets Gawain when he comes to Hautdesert castle.

Suggested Essays Topics

1. Why does Gawain choose All Souls' Day as the time to begin his journey? Look up the history of the holiday, and try to determine why it is significant.

2. Verse 24 tells us that Arthur provided a rich feast for the departure of Gawain, but the poem does not tell us what, if anything, he said to the young knight. What do you think this might have been? What do you think the king is feeling?

3. Gawain is particularly dedicated to the Virgin Mary, whose image is etched on the inside of his shield. Why does he pray to her rather than to Christ?

4. Research the history and meaning of the pentangle. Why has this been chosen as the symbol of Gawain?

5. Gawain, as the Knight of the Pentangle, has very high standards to uphold. Since all human beings are fallible, perhaps these standards are unrealistic? Perhaps Gawain demands too much of himself? What do you think?

Verses 35-45 (Lines 811-1125)

New Characters:

Lord Bertilak: *Lord of Hautdesert Castle who welcomes Gawain, and who will be later revealed as the Green Knight (not actually named until the end of the poem, but we will use this name earlier for convenience)*

Lady Bertilak: *the wife of Lord Bertilak, notable for her great beauty, who will later attempt to seduce Gawain*

Old Crone: *a woman who accompanies Lady Bertilak, and is as ugly as her companion is beautiful; occupies the place of honor at the celebrations, and later turns out to be the sorceress Morgan le Fay*

Summary

The porter who has come to greet Gawain at the castle invokes the name of St. Peter. He then hurries off, and servants come to help Gawain take off his armor. Soon the lord of the castle, Bertilak comes to welcome Gawain, saying he may stay and treat everything in the castle as his own.

Lord Bertilak is an unusually large man with a bright beard the color of a beaver's pelt. Gracious but fierce, he leads Gawain to a place by the fire, surrounded by splendor and luxury. When the master of the house learns that his guest is Gawain, he laughs with pleasure.

After dining, Gawain meets Lady Bertilak, who is exceedingly beautiful, even lovelier, Gawain thinks, than Queen Guinevere. Lady Bertilak, however, is accompanied by an old crone, who is as ugly as her partner is beautiful. Gawain politely bows to the older woman, then he lightly embraces the younger one and gives him a polite kiss. He pledges his service to both of them. After pleasant entertainments, Gawain goes to bed.

The next day, there is a feast. Gawain is paired with Lady Bertilak, while the old crone sits in the place of highest honor. Lady Bertilak and Gawain engage in lively conversation, but say and do nothing improper.

After the celebration, Bertilak leads Gawain to a chamber for the night. The lord of the castle tells Gawain that the visit is an honor, and he is welcome to stay longer. Gawain replies that he cannot stay, since he must find the Green Chapel within three days. Bertilak tells Gawain not to worry, since the place is just a short distance away.

Bertilak tells Gawain that he plans to hunt the next day. Gawain, he says, tired from the journey, should sleep late. Lady Bertilak then will keep him company when he takes his meal. Finally, Bertilak proposes a bargain. He will give Gawain whatever game he brings back from the hunt. Gawain, for his part, shall give Bertilak anything he obtains during the day. Gawain heartily agrees, then goes to bed.

Analysis

The porter who welcomes Gawain at Hautdesert Castle invokes the name of Saint Peter. The symbolism here is ambivalent. Peter was the keeper of the gate to heaven, but he was also guilty of denying Christ three times (the number of times that Gawain will later be tempted). While the place is certainly wondrous, the implicit comparison to heaven is partly ironic. Hautdesert Castle is similar to Camelot, which certainly appeared magnificent but was actually troubled.

One message here is that one should look beyond appearance. Everything, Gawain will learn later, is not what he imagined. Everyone from Lord and Lady Bertilak to the courtiers is constantly referring to the great reputation of Gawain, but that is flattery designed to lead him astray. Gawain may think he is only being entertained at Hautdesert Castle, but he is constantly being tested.

Despite the warmth which Gawain is received, there are many subtle hints of danger. Bertilak, who turns out later to be the Green Knight, has a beard the hue of a beaver's pelt. This is an animal that cuts down trees, and the neck of Gawain is about to be placed under the ax. When Bertilak learns of the identity of his guest (something he probably knew to begin with), he laughs. If the reader already suspects that Bertilak is the Green Knight, the laughter will appear sinister. The exchange which Bertilak proposes to his guest at the end of this section is reminiscent of the agreement between Gawain and the Green Knight.

There are also subtle hints of seductiveness in the description of Lady Bertilak. She is compared with Guinevere, who, according to legend, was guilty of adultery. Furthermore, the narrator assures the reader that there was nothing improper in the conversation between Gawain and Lady Bertilak, hinting at potential for an affair.

Finally, there is the presence of the mysterious old crone, whom we will later learn is Morgan le Fay. She never says a word, but her power and importance is obvious. In another medieval tale, *Sir Gawain and Dame Ragnall*, Gawain is romantically involved with a sorceress, who appears before him alternately as an old crone and a beautiful young lady. Lady Bertilak and the old crone are closely associated, and, especially for readers familiar with that story, they can seem like different aspects of the one human being. Medieval writers and artists liked to remind people of mortality and physical decay. The author may be saying that the beautiful young woman and the old crone are the same person at different stages of the life cycle.

The actual nature of Hautdesert Castle, however, will remain a mystery even at the end of the poem. None of the people there apart from Bertilak and Morgan le Fay is ever actually named in the poem, and they do not seem entirely real. The place is certainly uncanny, but we never know whether it is a genuine castle or simply a magical illusion. Perhaps it represents the dreams of glory which can be so seductive to a romantic young man.

Study Questions

1. Where do the courtiers take Gawain on his arrival at Hautdesert Castle?

2. What color is the beard of Lord Bertilak?

3. Where does Gawain go after meeting Bertilak?

4. Who accompanies Lady Bertilak when she goes to meet Gawain?

5. Who is paired with Gawain at mealtime on the day after his arrival at Hautdesert Castle?

6. Who sits in the place of highest honor at mealtime on the day after Gawain's arrival at Hautdesert Castle?

7. Why does Gawain, at first, not accept the invitation to stay longer at the castle?

8. How long does Gawain agree to stay at Hautdesert Castle?

9. What, according his agreement with Bertilak, will Gawain receive?

10. What, according to his agreement with Bertilak, must Gawain give in return?

Answers

1. The courtiers take Gawain into the main hall after he arrives at Hautdesert Castle.

2. The beard of Lord Bertilak is the hue of a beaver's pelt.

3. After meeting Bertilak, Gawain goes to a splendid room to change clothes.

4. An old crone accompanies Lady Bertilak when she goes to meet Gawain.

5. Lady Bertilak is paired with Gawain at mealtime on the day of his arrival at Hautdesert Castle.

6. The old crone sits in the place of highest honor at mealtime on the day after Gawain's arrival at Hautdesert Castle.

7. Gawain does not accept the invitation to stay longer, because he has little time to find the Green Chapel.

8. Gawain agrees to stay at Hautdesert Castle for three days.

9. According to his agreement with Bertilak, Gawain will receive whatever game Bertilak brings back from hunting.

10. According to his agreement with Bertilak, Gawain must give Bertilak whatever he obtains during the day.

Suggested Essays Topics

1. The narrator says that the beard of Bertilak is the hue of a beaver's pelt. What color, exactly, would that be? How might the color be significant?

2. Compare and contrast Camelot at the start of the poem with Hautdesert Castle. What do you think is the relation between the two?

3. Hautdesert Castle seems strange indeed, yet Gawain, to our knowledge, never enquires about either the castle or Bertilak. Why do you think he neglects to do this?

4. Gawain tells his host that he must find the Green Chapel, yet he never tells why. The host, for his part, never asks. Why do you think this is so?

SECTION FOUR

Part Three

Verses 46-66 (Lines 1126-1647)

Summary

Bertilak leads his followers on a hunt for venison. The stags are spared in accord with the season, but the hinds are driven into valleys, then shot with arrows. Those few that manage to escape are killed by the hounds.

Meanwhile, Gawain lingers in bed. Lady Bertilak enters his room, bolts the door. At first, he pretends to be asleep. She pulls the curtain from the canopy of his bed and watches him. After lying still for a considerable time, Gawain decides it would be best to speak to Lady Bertilak, opens his eyes and pretends to be amazed. Lady Bertilak speaks to him very seductively, reminding Gawain that Bertilak and the others are away. Then she openly offers her body to Gawain.

Gawain pretends not to understand, managing to reject the advances without offending the hostess. He repudiates the flattery of Lady Bertilak, saying that her husband is better than he. Finally, she says that he could not truly be Gawain, for such a renowned man would not have lingered with a lady without craving a kiss. Gawain replies that, to avoid offending her, he will give her the kiss, in accordance with the rules of courtesy. They exchange a kiss, and Lady Bertilak leaves. Gawain dresses and goes to mass. He spends the afternoon in civilized conversation with Lady Bertilak and the old crone.

Meanwhile, at the hunt, the hinds are piled up. They are systematically butchered, and the parts are ceremoniously divided among the participants in the hunt, from Lord Bertilak to the hounds. They return as it grows dark.

Bertilak brings all of the venison he has obtained to Gawain, who is very impressed. According to their agreement, he gives all of the game to Gawain. The guest, for his part, gives Bertilak the kiss he received, saying that is all he obtained. Bertilak thanks Gawain, then asks how he got the kiss. Gawain cleverly replies that he need not answer, for that was not in the agreement. Both laugh, and they go to supper.

The next day, Bertilak and his retinue hunt an enormous boar. This animal kills several hounds, and arrows fail to pierce its hide. The hunters, however, continue the pursuit.

At the same time, Gawain lingers again in bed. Once more, Lady Bertilak approaches him. This time she is even more sexually aggressive than before. She rebukes Gawain for lack of courtesy, because he refused her advances. This time Gawain is more direct in his refusal, and tells her to take back what she has said. She replies that Gawain is so strong that, even if she were so rude as to resist him, he would be able to force his will. Gawain replies that bullying is not admired in his country. Lady Bertilak continues her attempt to seduce Gawain, alternating flattery with taunts. Finally, after giving Gawain two kisses, she gives up and leaves.

Bertilak, meanwhile, is still pursuing the boar, which darts into a hole by a stream. The other hunters, many of whom have been wounded, are afraid to approach it. The master of the castle, however, dismounts and stalks the boar with his sword. They battle in the water until Bertilak kills the beast.

After the boar is disemboweled, Bertilak takes it home and presents it to Gawain. To fulfill his side of the bargain, Gawain gives Bertilak the two kisses he received. The lord of the castle expresses satisfaction.

Analysis

Critics and scholars have especially high praise for part three of *Sir Gawain and the Green Knight*, because of the sophisticated construction of the plot. Scenes of the hunt alternate with scenes of

the castle, suggesting many parallels between the two places. This technique also enables the author to communicate many emotional nuances through contrasting the activity indoors and outside.

Hunting was a fundamental part of life among the medieval aristocracy. Not only the men but also ladies frequently took part. Not only did hunting serve a variety of practical purposes beyond the obtaining of food, but it also was overlaid with many social and symbolic meanings.

For one thing, hunting supplied training for knights in the art of war. Additionally, it was a cooperative activity, which united a great many people together in common endeavor. Perhaps most significantly, hunting provided drama and excitement in times of peace. It involved not only vigorous physical activity but also a chance to display colorful costumes and pageantry. Stories of the hunt during the day would be recounted in the evening around the fire.

Hunting also reaffirmed the social order. As readers of the Robin Hood stories are aware, hunting large animals such as deer was strictly forbidden to common people, and poaching could be punished by death or mutilation. Everything from the assignment of tasks to the division of game was done very ceremoniously, in accord with the rank of people at the court. Furthermore, hunting was used, just as it sometimes is today, as a metaphor for amorous pursuit.

Most frequently, medieval people thought of the man as the hunter and the woman as game, but this time roles are reversed. Just as Bertilak is chasing animals, Lady Bertilak is after Gawain. The frequent changes of scene illuminate the analogies between the two pursuits.

The reversal of gender roles between Gawain and Lady Bertilak is especially stressed on the first day. In accord with the season, the hunters leave the stags and pursue only the hinds. This is subtly suggestive of adultery or, perhaps, even rape. Meanwhile, Gawain behaves less like a strong man than like a frightened hind, cowering in bed and pretending to be asleep.

Lady Bertilak, however, certainly does not seem to be fooled, and she repeatedly taunts the guest by saying he cannot truly be Gawain. These bedroom scenes test not only Gawain's sense of

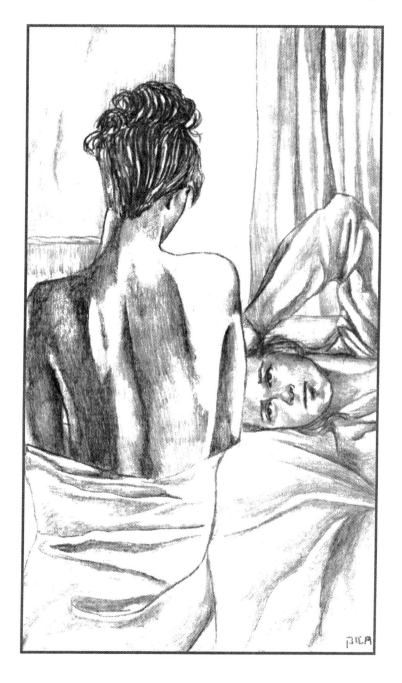

honor but also his wit and his social skills. He must reject the advances of his hostess without offending her, and he manages this with great virtuosity.

When Bertilak comes back with great piles of carcasses and gives them to Gawain, this is more than a display of generosity. The master of the castle is showing off his ability to kill, particularly to slaughter "hinds" such as Gawain. Rich as the spoils of the hunt may be, they are obviously of no possible use to Gawain. He certainly cannot eat it all, nor will he be able to take so much with him when he travels to the Green Chapel. Finally, all this wealth of food can only serve as a reminder that Gawain faces death in a few days.

Just as Gawain could not acknowledge the advances of the lady, he is unable to respond to the implicit threats of Bertilak. Once more, both his honor and his social graces are being tested. This time Gawain comes up with a very ingenious solution to a seemingly hopeless dilemma.

The kiss which Lady Bertilak gave to Gawain expressed at least as much aggression as affection. The kiss which Gawain gives Bertilak, after receiving it from the lady, is also ambiguous, especially since Gawain will not openly say how he received it. Both gifts, in their respective ways, are an expression of power. Gawain manages to stand up to Bertilak, just as he did to the lady, without being offensive.

The kiss, of course, is just as useless to Bertilak as the pile of game was to Gawain. Nevertheless, Bertilak professes to be pleased. We never know what he is really thinking, but he probably is sincere in admiration of Gawain's honesty and cleverness.

We are also unsure what the hero of the story is thinking. He seems naive and innocent, particularly since he appears not to notice anything strange about Hautdesert Castle. In spite of this, his handling of extremely difficult social situations suggests that he is actually becoming very shrewd. Perhaps he may even have begun to suspect that Bertilak is really the Green Knight?

The wild boar was an animal famed for its fighting spirit. Many medieval families painted boars on their crests to symbolize their fierceness. The hunters, led by Bertilak, are initially unable to overpower the boar. They finally kill the beast by provoking it to rage and wearing it down. This is the same tactic that Lady Bertilak uses on Gawain during his second day at Hautdesert Castle.

This time, Gawain is tested even more severely. Lady Bertilak is more aggressive than before, and Gawain is unable to play at being innocent of her designs. This time he challenges her openly, saying she should take back her remarks. She attempts to use his anger toward her purposes, provoking Gawain to greater aggressiveness and saying that she could not resist him even if she wished to. Gawain, however, proves not only brave as the boar but subtle as well. Unlike the beast, he refuses to be drawn into open combat, and he extricates himself from the situation through a combination of firmness and verbal skill.

When Bertilak gives Gawain the carcass of the enormous boar, the present is just as useless but even more threatening than the previous one. This time Gawain gives Bertilak not one kiss but two. The exchange illustrates the combination of fellowship and rivalry that is often found among those in activities which are traditionally considered very masculine such as, for example, rough athletic competitions.

Study Questions

1. What sounds accompany the hunt?

2. Do Bertilak and his men kill all of the deer?

3. What does Gawain first do when Lady Bertilak first enters his chamber?

4. Why does Lady Bertilak tell the guest that he cannot really be Gawain?

5. What does Gawain say on seeing the game that Bertilak brought back after the first day of hunting?

6. What does Bertilak give Gawain according to their agreement when he returns from the first day of hunting?

7. What does Gawain give Bertilak according to their agreement after his first day in the castle?

8. Why can the huntsmen not kill the boar with arrows?

9. How and by whom is the boar finally killed?

10. What does Gawain give Bertilak in exchange for the boar?

Answers

1. Horns and the barking of dogs are some of the sounds which accompany the hunt.

2. No, Bertilak and his men leave the stags and kill only the hinds.

3. When Lady Bertilak first enters his chamber, Gawain pretends to be asleep.

4. She says that the guest cannot be Gawain, because a knight like Gawain would not have stayed with a lady so long without claiming a kiss.

5. When Gawain sees the game that Bertilak brought back from the first day of hunting, he says that it is the finest harvest of game during the season that he has seen in seven years.

6. According to their agreement, Bertilak gives Gawain the piles of game that he obtained during the first day of hunting?

7. According to their agreement, Gawain gives Bertilak the kiss he received from the mistress of the house during his first day in the castle.

8. The huntsmen cannot kill the boar with arrows, because they fail to penetrate the hide.

9. The boar is finally killed by Bertilak with his sword.

10. In exchange for the boar, Gawain gives Bertilak the two kisses he received from Lady Bertilak during the day.

Suggested Essay Topics

1. Common methods of seduction have hardly changed at all since the Middle Ages. Both men and women are still led into relationships they do not want or believe are wrong through precisely the methods used by Lady Bertilak on Gawain. Young people often are not sure how to say "no," and the behavior of Gawain may still be an excellent model

for this in certain situations. Compare the seduction "lines"
used by Lady Bertilak with those that are common today.

2. The hunting scenes are probably described in more realis-
   tic detail than anything else in *Sir Gawain and the Green
   Knight*. What do you think might be the reason for this?

3. What do you think might have happened if Gawain had let
   himself be seduced by Lady Bertilak?

4. The verbal ploys of Lady Bertilak are very similar to those of
   the Green Knight when he first visited the court of Arthur.
   The Green Knight got Arthur to accept his strange challenge
   by taunting Arthur and his knights with cowardice (Saying,
   in effect, "What's wrong? Are you chicken?"). Lady Bertilak
   tries the same thing on Gawain, but it does not work. Does
   this mean that Arthur succumbed to a temptation while
   Gawain withstood it?

5. Almost all readers assume that Gawain does not suspect that
   Bertilak is the Green Knight, but we can see that Gawain is
   pretty clever. Perhaps he suspects this after all. If so, why does
   he say nothing? Suppose that he did suspect and said to
   Bertilak directly: "I think you're the Green Knight." What
   might have happened then?

Verses 67-79 (Lines 1648-1997)

Summary

Over dinner, Gawain is engaged in conversation with Lady
Bertilak. After festivities, Gawain tells Bertilak that he wishes to
depart in the morning, but Bertilak urges him to stay one more
night. They should not let the opportunity for enjoyment pass, he
urges, for the future is uncertain. Gawain agrees and, once again,
lingers in bed the next morning.

The next day, the lord of the castle chases a fox. It tries to elude
the hounds by changing direction and taking unexpected paths.
At times the fox appears to elude the party, but they take up the
trail again.

Meanwhile, the mistress of the house comes, once again, to Gawain's bed, wearing a splendid robe. She finds him unsettled, troubled by dreams about his appointment with the Green Knight, and bends over to give him a kiss. Gawain gently repulses her advance. She asks if he is so restrained because he has another love. Gawain replies that is not so.

At this, the lady is abashed. Giving up the idea of seducing Gawain, she asks for a token to remember him by. Gawain replies that he has nothing worthy to give, since he has not taken any baggage with him on the journey. The lady replies that she, in that case, will give something to Gawain.

First, she offers him a precious ring. Gawain refuses it, saying that, since he can give nothing in return he can also not accept anything. Lady Bertilak replies that perhaps, the ring is too valuable, so a less costly gift would be more appropriate. She offers him her green sash instead. When Gawain refuses that as well, she says that it has magical properties and can preserve the wearer from weapons. Thinking the sash might protect him from the Green Knight, Gawain at last accepts. The lady implores Gawain not to tell her husband about the sash. He agrees, and she leaves after having given Gawain a total of three kisses.

Gawain dresses, and goes to the chapel to confess, preparing to be beheaded by the Green Knight. The priest absolves him of his sins. He then joins in the Christmas festivities.

While this takes place, the party is still following the fox. Bertilak waits in ambush, then throws his sword in front of the fox. Before the animal can turn, the dogs seize it.

When Bertilak returns, Gawain does not wait to find out what he has brought. Gawain greets Bertilak, giving him the three kisses he received but saying nothing about the sash. Bertilak says, regretfully, that he has only a paltry fox-pelt to give in exchange, then tells Gawain how the fox was slain.

After the meal and festivities, Gawain asks Bertilak to provide him with a guide to the Green Chapel the next morning, and the lord of the castle agrees. He says farewell to the lords and ladies of Hautdesert Castle, then sleeps uneasily thorough the final night before setting out.

Analysis

During the eighteenth century, when hunting deer was no longer the exclusive privilege of the nobility, they turned to the fox hunt for recreation. In the Middle Ages, however, the lords and ladies generally hunted large animals such as deer, while hunting foxes was generally left to the common people. Such game was considered unworthy of a knight. People probably found the idea of a huge party with dogs pursuing a little fox to be a bit ridiculous, just as some do today.

Nevertheless, the spectacle corresponds, once again, to the behavior of Gawain. Just as the fox constantly swerves and changes direction to avoid capture, Gawain is wavering and irresolute. In the morning, his sleep is troubled by the thought of his imminent execution by the Green Knight. The expectation that he is about to die makes the temptations more intense. Gawain can no longer postpone enjoyments, but, he believes, must have them at once or not at all.

When Gawain tells the mistress of the house that he is not pledged to any other woman, nor does he expect to be for a time, she takes that as a final rebuff of her attempt at seduction. The reason is not immediately clear. This could mean that she was looking for an affair without commitment, and wished for somebody pledged to another woman.

As we learn later in the poem, however, Lady Bertilak knows about Gawain's appointment with the Green Knight. Perhaps, then, the declaration of Gawain tells her that he has accepted the finality of death and all the loss it entails. This explanation certainly does more credit to both parties.

Lady Bertilak changes her approach and asks Gawain for a gift to remember him by. In view of his expected death, the request seems ironic. The temptation here is renown, prized by the ancient warriors. Thinking back on the founders of dynasties mentioned in the opening lines of the poem, we will recall that posthumous fame was often linked with dishonor. Unlike Aeneas and many others, Gawain places integrity above that sort of immortality.

The temptation of the ring may be that of wealth. Gawain, however, realizes that he cannot take riches with him to the grave.

The last temptation, the green sash, however, is the most subtle. It is the idea that, through trickery, a person may evade fate.

After initially refusing the green sash, he takes it from Lady Bertilak in hope of saving his life. He then conceals this from Bertilak. After Bertilak throws his sword to block the way of the fox, the fox, uncertain which way to turn, is killed through irresolution. It loses time, and is caught by the dogs. Possibly the sword thrown by Bertilak might be compared with the belt, offered by the mistress of the house as a last resort after her other schemes had failed.

On the previous days, Gawain had waited for Bertilak to present his winnings before offering the kisses he received. This time, Gawain takes the initiative and gives Bertilak the kisses at once. This might be a way to evade questions. Bertilak gives Gawain the fox pelt, and tells how the animal was slain. Gawain, once more, does not reciprocate by telling how the kisses were obtained.

Though Gawain has taken the green sash, his subsequent behavior suggests that he does not have a great deal of confidence in its power. He then confesses and prepares himself for death. We do not know whether he confesses taking the sash or whether he fully realizes that he has done something wrong.

Study Questions

1. What is on Gawain's mind when Lady Bertilak enters his chamber on the third day?

2. What does Lady Bertilak do after entering Gawain's chamber for the third time?

3. After she has given up her attempt at seduction, what does the mistress of the house request of Gawain?

4. What does the mistress of the house offer to Gawain first after he has declined to give her a token to remember him by?

5. What does the mistress of the house say her green sash can accomplish?

6. What does Gawain do after he has taken the green sash?

7. What does Bertilak do after the fox has been killed?

8. What does Gawain give Bertilak in exchange for the fox pelt?

9. What final request does Gawain make of Bertilak?

10. What is the last thing Gawain does before going to bed?

Answers

1. Gawain is drowsing uneasily, troubled by dreams of his appointment with the Green Knight, when Lady Bertilak enters his chamber on the third day.

2. After entering Gawain's chamber for the third time, Lady Bertilak bends over Gawain and gives him a kiss.

3. After she has given up her attempt at seduction, the mistress of the house asks Gawain for a token to remember him by.

4. After he has declined to give her a token to remember him by, the mistress of the house first offers Gawain a precious ring.

5. The mistress of the house says her green sash can protect the wearer from being harmed by weapons.

6. After he has taken the green sash, Gawain goes to mass and confesses his sins.

7. After the fox has been killed, Bertilak holds up the fox to display it. Then he has the animal skinned.

8. In exchange for the fox pelt, Gawain gives Bertilak the three kisses he received from the mistress of the house.

9. The final request that Gawain makes of Bertilak is for a guide to the Green Chapel.

10. The last thing that Gawain does before going to bed is to say farewell to the members of Bertilak's household and thank them for their hospitality.

Suggested Essays Topics

1. In the context of the poem, it is considered honorable for Gawain to exchange gifts with Bertilak but dishonorable to exchange gifts with Bertilak's wife. Why do you think this is so?

2.   Compare the fox hunt in *Sir Gawain and the Green Knight* with modern descriptions of the fox hunt, for example in John Masefield's long poem *Reynard the Fox*. How have the technique and the meaning of the fox hunt changed?

3.   Today most people are accustomed to buying their meat in the supermarket and are shielded from any experience of killing or butchering. The hunt scenes in *Sir Gawain and the Green Knight* will impress many people as bloody at least. Do you believe they are cruel? Do you think the Gawain poet intended them as examples of cruelty? Explain your answers.

4.   Was Gawain telling the mistress of the house the truth when he said that he had no token to give her? What do you think might have happened if he had given her a token?

5.   Even with the green sash, Gawain appears to have almost no confidence about surviving the meeting with the Green Knight. How much confidence do you think he has in the magical power of the sash? What reasons does he have to believe in this magic? What reasons does he have to disbelieve in it?

Part Four

Verses 80-87 (Lines 1998-2211)

New Character:

Gawain's Guide: *servant who accompanies Gawain from the castle Haupdesert to the Green Knight*

Summary

Gawain awakes on a bleak, snowy day. After summoning his guide to take him to the Green Chapel, he puts on his armor. Along with his coat, he wraps the green sash about him, then sets out on what he thinks will be his final journey.

As they approach the Green Chapel, the guide tells Gawain that he dares go no further. The Green Knight, he tells Gawain, is known for his fierceness and his cruelty. No man, the guide says, can stand up to the Green Knight in battle, and everyone who goes to the Green Chapel is killed.

The guide himself, he tells Gawain, dares to go no further. He advises Gawain as well to turn back, and says he will keep it a secret if Gawain does, even if he must swear solemnly to the lie. Though irritated, Gawain thanks the guide for his good wishes. He then declines the offer and insists on going on.

The guide gives Gawain a lance and helmet, then directs him to descend alone into a ravine. He hurries away, leaving Gawain to face the Green Knight alone. Gawain follows the path into a grim and desolate place, filled with huge, jagged rocks.

He comes to a large mound beside a stream. Dismounting, he tethers his horse to a tree. Approaching he finds a cavern, which, he thinks, could be a pagan temple.

Analysis

Mounds in pre-Christian Britain and Ireland were often places of worship. In the folklore of the British Isles, they were dwelling places of fairies. These ambiguous creatures were considered capable of either generosity or cruelty.

Fairies were sometimes identified with both fallen angels, ghosts or pagan nature-spirits. While Victorian representations generally made fairies small, older folkloric descriptions made them the size of mortals or larger. At times they would be green like the adversary of Gawain.

Folkloric traditions concerning fairies vary widely, but they are very consistent about one thing—that is almost always best to avoid contact with them. Fairies, while not necessarily either good or evil, are very powerful and unpredictable. They live by codes which are very different from those of ordinary mortals. There are many stories of people who were destroyed by contact with fairies and others of people who barely escaped, but there are very few stories of people who received any lasting benefit from such contact.

The guide is, perhaps, a vehicle for folkloric traditions. He does not seem to share or even understand the knightly code of Gawain, according to which both cowardice and breaking of one's word are very severe violations of honor. As we will learn shortly, however, he is also part of an attempt to test Gawain. It may be that he does not believe what he says and is simply trying to frighten Gawain on orders from Bertilak, who, we shall learn shortly, is the Green Knight.

Study Questions

1. How is the weather when Gawain awakes to journey to the Green Chapel?

2. What does Gawain wear for the final journey to the Green Chapel?

3. How does Gawain travel to the Green Chapel?

4. Who sees Gawain off when he leaves Hautdesert Castle?

5. What does Gawain think to himself as he leaves Hautdesert Castle?

6. What does the guide tell Gawain about the Green Knight?

7. What does the guide urge Gawain to do?

8. What does the guide do after warning Gawain about the Green Knight?

9. Where does the path the guide pointed out take Gawain?

10. What does Gawain find after he dismounts?

Answers

1. The weather is bleak and snowy when Gawain wakes to journey to the Green Chapel.

2. The things Gawain wears for his final journey to the Green Chapel include armor, a coat, and the green sash from the mistress of the house.

3. Gawain travels to the Green Chapel on his horse Gringolet.

4. Only the porter sees Gawain off when he leaves Hautdesert Castle.

5. As he leaves Hautdesert Castle, Gawain thinks to himself how well the people there have treated him and that they deserve to be rewarded.

6. The guide tells Gawain that the Green Knight is mighty and has no mercy.

7. The guide urges Gawain to turn back and not go to the Green Chapel.

8. After warning him about the Green Knight, the guide gives Gawain a lance and a helmet, then turns around and leaves.

9. The path the guide pointed out takes Gawain into a ravine.

10. After he dismounts, Gawain finds a mound that contains a cavern.

Suggested Essays Topics

1. Why are none of the lords and ladies at Hautdesert Castle present when Gawain leaves Hautdesert Castle in the morning?

2. Commoners did not share the elaborate knightly codes and probably could not understand them. What do you suppose the guide may think of Gawain?

3. Compare the landscape around the Green Chapel with other haunted places you know of from literature or popular culture. What natural features are common in depictions of such places?

4. The late medieval German artist Albrecht Dürer did a famous etching entitled *The Knight, Death and the Devil*, in which a knight resolutely rides forward to meet his fate, heedless of attempts to frighten him. Look up the etching, and compare the knight with Gawain on his way to the Green Chapel.

5. Compare the departure of Gawain from Hautdesert Castle with his departure from Camelot.

Verses 88-101 (Lines 2212-2630)

Summary

At first the mound seems deserted, and Gawain wonders if he has been led to the desolate place by the Devil himself. Then Gawain hears a whirring noise, an ax being sharpened. He calls out, and the Green Knight answers that he will come immediately to claim what he has been pledged.

The Green Knight emerges from a cavern in the mound, carrying a huge ax. Gawain tells the Green Knight to take only a single stroke, then bows his head. The Green Knight raises his ax. As the ax descends on his neck, Gawain flinches and looks up. The Green Knight suddenly checks the stroke, and says that his adversary is too cowardly to truly be Gawain. The man with the ax reminds Gawain that he, the Green Knight never flinched when his own head was cut off.

Gawain swears that he will not flinch again. He bows a second time and stands still as a tree. The Green Knight raises his ax once more, but he again brings it down without making contact. Gawain continues waiting until the Green Knight begins to taunt him.

When he realizes what happened, Gawain grows angry at the delay. He accuses the Green Knight of being afraid to deliver the blow. He bows his head for a third time. The Green Knight raises the ax and brings it down, wounding Gawain lightly on the neck but doing no serious damage.

When Gawain sees the blood in the snow, he leaps up, filled with new life. He quickly puts on his helmet, draws his sword and declares that he has fulfilled the contract, and will fight if the Green Knight delivers another blow.

The Green Knight replies in a friendly manner that Gawain has endured his stroke according to the contract and all further obligations are cancelled. The first two strokes, the Green Knight explains, were for the first two times when the mistress of Hautdesert Castle, his wife, came to Gawain's chamber. He checked the blows, since Gawain had withstood the temptation. The third blow, which nicked Gawain but did not hurt him, was for the third time. Gawain, the Green Knight explains, had withstood the other temptations, but the guest was dishonorable in taking the sash and keeping it from the lord of the castle.

The Green Knight explains that he and his wife were working together to test Gawain, and he had known of everything that happened all along. Gawain, though not perfect, had acquitted himself extremely well. Gawain, however, reproaches himself for cowardice and covetousness. He takes off the sash and tosses it back to the Green Knight.

The Green Knight replies that Gawain has absolved himself of any wrongdoing. He gives Gawain the sash as a gift and a souvenir of the adventure at the Green Chapel. Gawain, the Green Knight says, may think of it as he moves in the society of Camelot after his return. The Green Knight then invites Gawain to return to Hautdesert Castle for the festivities of New Year's Eve. His wife, the Green Knight continues, will treat him without deception, in spite of the way she tricked him before.

Gawain refuses the invitation politely, wishing well to the Green Knight, his wife and the old crone. He then compares his experience to that of other men corrupted by women: Adam taken in by Eve, Solomon by Sheba and others, Samson by Delilah and David by Bathsheba.

As for the sash, Gawain says, he will wear it, not for its beauty but as a check on excessive pride. Whenever he is tempted to bask in glory, the sash will remind of his shortcomings. Then Gawain asks the Green Knight, as a final favor, for his true name.

The Green Knight, giving the name for the first time, says he is Bertilak of Hautdesert Castle. The sorceress Morgan le Fay, the old crone who stays there, had learned her magic from the wizard Merlin. She enchanted him into the form of the Green Knight and sent him to deliver the challenge at Camelot. She wishes to amaze the court and to frighten Guinevere.

Morgan, Bertilak continues, is also the half-sister of Arthur and the aunt of Gawain. Once again, Bertilak invites Gawain to Hautdesert Castle, but the knight declines. They embrace, and Gawain rides home.

After returning to Camelot, Gawain wears the green sash, as promised, as a baldric covering the scar in his neck, in token of his shortcomings. He is warmly received. The men and women at court, however, take it as a sign of honor and renown. The knights all begin to wear bands of bright green to recall Gawain's great adventure.

Analysis

The happy ending of the story is emotionally satisfying though, at least for contemporary readers, it leaves a great many things unresolved. Several ideas emerge clearly, but no interpretation of the poem, especially the last part, has been able to account for all the details. With respect to his descriptive and narrative powers, the Gawain poet has few peers, but perhaps he was not terribly interested in thematic unity. It may also be that he deliberately left many things unresolved, to inspire his readers to think about them further.

One puzzle is the significance of the green sash that Gawain was given, first by Lady Bertilak and later by the Green Knight. The distinguished scholar of Arthurian legends believed that this was

truly magical and protected Gawain from the ax. He pointed out that many other Arthurian romances have tokens with similar power, sometimes, as in this story, a sash.

The vast majority of scholars, however, reject this interpretation. If it is correct, it is very hard to make either psychological or thematic sense of many details. If the sash was magical, how, for example, could we explain either Bertilak's rebuke to Gawain for violating their bargain or his subsequent gift of the sash to Gawain as a souvenir? Furthermore, Gawain himself never seemed to have much confidence in the protective power of the sash. Finally, when Gawain takes the sash as a gift from Bertilak, he does not even mention the idea of using it to protect himself in battle. On the contrary, Gawain appears to assume that the sash has no magic, and he is only concerned about what it will symbolize.

Very probably, the alleged magical power of the sash was a ruse, a final test of Gawain. This false claim of magic is certainly unusual in Arthurian romances. Most of them, *Sir Gawain and the Green Knight* included, are full of fantastic events. They assume complete credulity, or at least suspension of disbelief, on the part of the reader.

Yet the Gawain poet was certainly satirizing Arthur and his court, and perhaps he wished to gently make fun of Arthurian romances as well. For all his love of magical lore, he was a clearly shrewd and skeptical observer. An author with his powers of observation would be entirely capable of seeing through the foibles of his time. In the late fourteenth century when he wrote, the culture of chivalry was in decline, and the forms were being reduced to merely an elaborate system of etiquette.

The nick given to Gawain by the Green Knight has additional significance, since it occurs on January first, the Feast of Circumcision of the liturgical calendar. Circumcision is a wound that does not maim or kill, and it was thought of as an early form of baptism. Accordingly, Gawain rises from the blow filled with new life, as though reborn.

The motives of Bertilak and Morgan le Fay are harder to explain. Bertilak tells Gawain that Morgan le Fay had him appear at Camelot in the form of the Green Knight and issue his strange challenge to frighten Guinevere. This raises far more questions than it answers.

We do not know, for example, just why Morgan le Fay wishes to frighten Guinevere, and feminine rivalry is not a sufficient

explanation. There may well be references to stories here which were well-known in the late fourteenth century but have since been lost. The stated purpose of Morgan le Fay suggests, however, that she expected Guinevere's husband, King Arthur, rather than Gawain to take up the challenge of the Green Knight. Perhaps the original intent of the challenge was to bring Arthur, the half- sister of Morgan le Fay, to Hautdesert Castle. There is probably no way to tell.

Still more significantly, the stated motive of the sorceress does not explain why Bertilak, Lady Bertilak and Morgan le Fay herself went to such lengths to test Gawain. We may view these tests in many ways, for example as a rite of passage into full manhood. However, if the figures that tested Gawain are more than, say, indifferent powers of nature, we must look for their motivations.

The only hint of an explanation is the renewed invitation by the Green Knight to come to Hautdesert Castle for renewed festivities, which Gawain refuses. Perhaps Morgan le Fay and Bertilak wished to win Gawain for some scheme which would be directed against Guinevere and Camelot? Perhaps they simply took a familial interest in him, since Gawain had a blood tie with Morgan le Fay. The invitation could have been a simple expression of good will or else a last temptation. Gawain, understandably, elects not to take any more chances.

As Gawain refuses, he launches into a misogynistic diatribe, of a sort that seems uncharacteristic for him but which was very common during the late Middle Ages. He speaks of famous men who have been brought down by women: Adam, Solomon, Samson and David. The speech, like many in the poem, is probably somewhat satirical, and may represent simply an outburst of temper. Gawain, after all, may be wiser than at the beginning of the poem, but he is still a very human figure.

The entire poem is largely about personal responsibility, and Gawain himself, everywhere else, has declined to unload responsibility for his acts on to others. Furthermore, some of what he says is very obviously unfair, and the audience of the poem must have been aware of this. To blame Eve for the deeds of Adam may have at least some plausibility, but poor Bathsheba certainly did nothing that merits blame for the murder committed by David. Perhaps the poet wished to show that, though he does not realize it, Gawain has actually been far more honorable than the patriarchs of the

Old Testament. As soon as his anger has been vented, Gawain changes his tone, and expresses his affection for Morgan le Fay and Lady Bertilak of Hautdesert Castle.

Gawain agrees to wear the sash to commemorate his failure, as a check on excessive pride. Ironically, his companions at the Round Table assign it the opposite meaning, that in fact they imitate him. Some scholars believe this poem commemorates the origin of a brotherhood whose members wore a green baldric. This closing incident may also be a satire on fashion. The late fourteenth century was a period of transition from feudal to early capitalist society, when expansion of trade and greater efficiency of manu-facturing caused styles to change more rapidly.

The adoption of the green baldric as a fashion, like much in the poem, suggests the superficiality of the society of the Round Table. Arthur, his knights and ladies are unable to comprehend the lesson of humility. But perhaps the initial judgement of Gawain on himself was too severe, and the truth lies somewhere in between.

Study Questions

1. What does Gawain hear after he first arrives at the Green Chapel?
2. Where does the Green Knight first appear?
3. How does the Green Knight cross the stream?
4. What does Gawain ask after he has greeted the Green Knight?
5. What does Gawain do when the Green Knight first lowers the ax?
6. How does Gawain stand when the Green Knight lowers the ax a second time?
7. What does Gawain see after the Green Knight lowers the ax a third time?
8. For what does Gawain reproach himself?
9. What final request does Gawain make of the Green Knight?
10. What do Gawain and Bertilak do as the part company?

Answers

1. After he first arrives at the Green Chapel, Gawain hears the sharpening of an ax.

2. The Green Knight first appears above Gawain, on the opposite bank of the stream from him.

3. The Green Knight vaults over the stream on his ax.

4. After he has greeted the Green Knight, Gawain asks that the Green Knight cut off his head quickly with a single stroke.

5. When the Green Knight first lowers the ax, Gawain flinches and looks up.

6. Gawain stands still as a stump of a tree when the Green Knight lowers the ax a second time.

7. After the Green Knight lowers the ax a third time, Gawain sees his blood glittering in the snow.

8. Gawain reproaches himself for showing cowardice and covetousness by taking the sash offered him by Lady Bertilak.

9. The final request that Gawain makes of the Green Knight is to learn his true name.

10. As they part company, Gawain and Bertilak embrace and kiss.

Suggested Essay Topics

1. Bertilak, who is also the Green Knight, remains a mysterious figure even at the end of the poem. Do you think he is basically good, evil or fundamentally ambiguous?

2. Perhaps even more mysterious than Bertilak is Morgan le Fay. How do you think her presence changes the poem? What is her significance?

3. The words of Bertilak suggest that Morgan le Fay might have intended Arthur rather than Gawain to take up the original challenge of the Green Knight in Camelot. In light of what we now know about the Green Knight and Morgan le Fay,

what do you now think would have happened if Arthur, not Gawain, had beheaded the Green Knight? Do you think Arthur would have taken the journey to find the Green Chapel? Do you think he would have encountered Bertilak at Hautdesert Castle? Would Lady Bertilak have tested him? If these things had happened, do you think he would have acquitted himself as well as Gawain did?

4.   King Arthur and his court understand the meaning of the green sash very differently from the way Gawain does. Which way of understanding it do you think is more correct and appropriate?

5.   With his portrait of Camelot, the Gawain poet may have been satirizing the courts of his own time, the latter fourteenth century. He criticizes, among other things, the superficiality of the lords and ladies. Many of his implicit criticisms, such as an excessive preoccupation with fashion and glamour, could also be made of contemporary American society. How much do you think people have changed since the time of the Gawain poet?

Sample Analytical Paper Topics

These are topics on which you can write a substantial anaytical paper. They are designed to test your understanding of major themes and details from the work as a whole. Following the topics are outlines you can use as a starting point for writing an analytical paper.

Topic #1

The major theme of *Sir Gawain and the Green Knight* is the hero's passage to maturity. Along the way, he passes three major tests. First, he shows courage and initiative when he volunteers to take the place of Arthur and accept the challenge of the Green Knight. Second, he shows discipline, self-control and honor when he refuses the advances of Lady Bertilak. Third, he faces death when he keeps his appointment with the Green Knight. Review each of these episodes carefully, and notice the way Gawain changes.

When Gawain returns to Camelot after his adventure, his maturity seems to set him apart from his old companions, who are unable to understand what has happened. Something of the sort often happens to young people, who may outgrow their old companions. Have you ever had similar experiences? Can you think of anyone else who has?

Outline

I. Thesis Statement: *The major theme of* Sir Gawain and the Green Knight *is the passage to maturity of the hero, Sir Gawain.*

II. Introduction: Gawain and Camelot at the start of *Sir Gawain and the Green Knight*

III. The First Test: The challenge of the Green Knight

    A. What Gawain demonstrates

    B. What Gawain learns

IV. The Second Test: Withstanding the attempt at seduction

    A. What Gawain demonstrates

    B. What Gawain learns

V. The Third Test: Facing death

    A. What Gawain demonstrates

    B. What Gawain learns

VI. Conclusion: The return to Camelot

    A. How Gawain has matured

    B. Gawain and the society at Camelot

Topic #2

In *Sir Gawain and the Green Knight*, Arthur, Gawain and Bertilak/The Green Knight represent three respective visions of the medieval warrior. All three portraits are presented with some admiration, but none of them is entirely uncritical. Compare and contrast these three figures. By examining their strengths and weaknesses, decide what the Gawain poet thought of chivalry and its codes.

Outline

I. Thesis Statement: *Arthur, Gawain, and Bertilak/the Green Knight each represent three respective visions of the Medieval warroir, presented with some admiration, but none of them is entirely uncritical.*

II.   Introduction: The warrior ideal in the Middle Ages

III. The figure of Arthur in *Sir Gawain and the Green Knight*

   A.   The strengths of Arthur

   B.   The weaknesses of Arthur

IV. The figure of Bertilak/The Green Knight in *Sir Gawain and the Green Knight*

   A.   The strengths of Bertilak

   B.   The weaknesses of Bertilak

V.   The figure of Gawain in *Sir Gawain and the Green Knight*

   A.   The strengths of Gawain

   B.   The weaknesses of Gawain

VI. Conclusion: What the Gawain Poet thought of Chivalry

Topic #3

There is certainly a rich range of feminine models in *Sir Gawain and the Green Knight*, even though none of them are as fully developed as Sir Gawain or the Green Knight. All of them, without exception, are very powerful figures. Apart from the Virgin Mary, to whom Gawain is dedicated, all of them are also ambivalent, poised precariously between good and evil. The student will compare and contrast these various female figures, then see what, if anything, they reveal about the position of women in the late middle ages.

Outline

I.   Thesis Statement: *The female characters in* Sir Gawain and The Green Knight *Represent/do not represent the position of the women in the Middle Ages.*

II. Introduction: The changing roles of woman

III. Guinevere in *Sir Gawain and the Green Knight*

   A.   Guinevere as an inspiration

   B.   Guinevere as a temptress

IV.   Lady Bertilak in *Sir Gawain and the Green Knight*

     A.   Lady Bertilak as a temptress

     B.   Lady Bertilak as upholder of morality

V.   Morgan le Fay in *Sir Gawain and the Green Knight*

     A.   Morgan le Fay as a pagan goddess

     B.   Morgan le Fay as a force for good or evil

VI.   The View of Women in *Sir Gawain and the Green Knight*

     A.   The Misogenistic Attack on Women by Gawain (lines 2416 – 2422)

     B.   Gawain's veneration of Mary

     C.   Conclusion: The ambivalent roles of women

Topic #4

Three hunts are described in enormous detail in part four of *Sir Gawain and the Green Knight*. The poem is, for this reason, a very important document of both the methods and the social significance of hunting in the middle ages. The hunt is also used as a metaphor or sexual pursuit when Lady Bertilak attempts to seduce Gawain.

Read the hunting scenes carefully. Note how the hunt was conducted and the emotions surrounding it. Then analyze, in as much detail as possible, the ways in which hunting is used as a metaphor for love or sex.

Outline

I.   Thesis Statement: *Hunting is used as a metaphor in* Sir Gawain and the Green Knight.

II.   Introduction: Love, Sex, Violence and Hunting

     A.   Hunting as an act of violence

     B.   The hunt as a metaphor for sexual aggression

III. The hunt of Deer in *Sir Gawain and the Green Knight*

     A.   The Stag as the King of the Forest

     B.   How the Stag tries to escape by running

    C.   How Lady Bertilak tried to seduce Sir Gawain during his first day in Hautdesert Castle

    D.   How Gawain was like a stag

    E.   The first exchange between Sir Gawain and Lord Bertilak

    F.   The high value placed on the Stag

IV. The hunt of the boar in *Sir Gawain and the Green Knight*

    A.   The boar as a symbol of fieceness

    B.   How the stag tries to escape by fighting

    C.   How Lady Bertilak tried to seduce Gawain during his second day in Hautdesert Castle

    D.   How Gawain was like a boar

    E.   The second exchange between Sir Gawain and Lord Bertilak

    F.   The high value placed on the boar

V. The hunt of the fox in *Sir Gawain and the Green Knight*

    A.   The fox as a symbol of deception

    B.   How the fox tries to escape by changing course and trickery

    C.   How Lady Bertilak tried to seduce Gawain during his third day in Hautdesert Castle

    D.   How Gawain was like a fox

    E.   The third exchange between Sir Gawain and Lord Bertilak

    F.   The low value placed on the fox

VI. The hunt as a metaphor in *Sir Gawain and the Green Knight*

    A.   The parallels between Lord Bertilak's hunting and Lady Bertilak's attempt at seduction

    B.   How the hunt combines sex and violence

    C.   Conclusion: The cultural meaning of the hunt

Bibliography

Anderson, William. *Green Man: The Archetype of our Oneness with the Earth.* San Francisco: HarperCollins, 1990.

Bechmann, Roland. *Trees and Man: The Forest in the Middle Ages.* Trans. from the French by Katharyn Dunham. New York: Paragon House, 1990.

Boroff, Marie. *Sir Gawain and the Green Knight: A Stylistic and Metrical Study.* New Haven: Yale U. Press, 1962.

Borroff, Marie, trans. *Sir Gawain and the Green Knight.* New York: Norton, 1967.

Briggs, Katherine. *The Vanishing People: Fairy Lore and Legends.* New York: Pasntheon, 1988.

Burrow, J. A. & Thorlac Turville-Petre. *A Book of Middle English.* Cambridge, Mass.: Blackwell, 1994.

Cartmill, Matt. *A View to a Death in the Morning: Hunting and Nature through History.* Cambridge: Harvard U. Press, 1993.

Clein, Wendy. *Concepts of Chivalry in Sir Gawain and the Green Knight.* Norman, Ok: Pilgrim, 1987.

Cosman, Madeleine Pelner. *Fabulous Feasts: Medieval Cookery and Ceremony.* New York: Braziller, 1976.

Davenport, W. A. *The Art of the Gawain Poet.* London: Athlone, 1978.

Dickson, Arthur. *Valentine and Orson: A Study in Late Medieval Romance.* New York: Oxford U. Press, 1929.

Ferrante, Joan M. and George D. Economu, eds. *In Pursuit of Perfection: Courtly Love in Medieval Literature.* Port Washington: Kennikat, 1975.

Gantz, Jeffrey, ed. & trans. *Early Irish Myths and Sagas.* New York: Penguin, 1982.

Haines, Victor Yelverton. *The Fortunate Fall of Sir Gawain: The Typology of Sir Gawain and the Green Knight.* Washington, D. C.: UPA, 1982.

Johnson, Lynn Staley. *The Voice of the Gawain Poet.* Madison: U. of Wisconsin Press, 1984.

Loomis, Roger Sherman. *Studies in Medieval Literature: A Memorial Collection of Essays.* New York: Burt Franklin, 1970.

Mathews, John. *Gawain: Knight of the Goddess.* London: Aquarian Press, 1990.

Miller, Mariam Youngerman & Jane Chance, eds. *Approaches to Teaching Sir Gawain and the Green Knight.* New York: MLA, 1986.

Perlin, John. A *Forest Journey: The Role of Wood in the Development of Civilization.* Cambridge, Mass.: Harvard U. Press,1989.

Sax, Boria. *The Frog King: On Fables, Fairy Tales and Legends of Animals.* New York: Pace U. Press, 1990.

Schama, Simon. *Landscape and Memory.* New York: Knopf, 1995.

Shahar, Shulamith. *The Fourth Estate: A history of women in the Middle Ages.* London: Routledge, 1993.

Shoaf, R. A. *The Poem as a Green Girdle: Commercialism in Sir Gawain and the Green Knight.* Gainsville, Fl.: U. Press of Florida, 1984.

Stone, Brian, trans. *Sir Gawain and the Green Knight.* New York: Penguin, 1988.

Thibaux, Marcelle. *The Stag of Love: The Chase in Medieval Literature.* Ithaca: Cornell U. Press, 1974.

Tolkien, J. R. R. and E. V. Gordon, eds. *Sir Gawain and the Green Knight.* New York: Oxford U. Press, 1967.

Watson, Henry, trans. *Valentine and Orson.* Ed. by Arthur Dickson. New York: Kraus Reprints, 1971 (first published 1503-95).

Weston, Jessie L. *From Ritual to Romance.* New York: Doubleday, 1957

THE BEST TEST PREPARATION FOR THE

AP
ADVANCED
PLACEMENT
EXAMINATION

ENGLISH
Literature & Composition

by Pauline Beard, Ph.D. • Robert Liftig, Ed.D. • James Mohr, Ph.D. •
James Maloney, M.A. • Joanne Miller, M.A. • Peter Trenouth, M.A. • Mattie Williams, M.A.

6 Full-Length Exams
➤ Every question based on the current exams
➤ The ONLY test preparation book with detailed explanations to every question
➤ Far more comprehensive than any other test preparation book

Includes a COMPREHENSIVE AP COURSE REVIEW,
emphasizing all areas of literature & composition found on the exam

R&A *Research & Education Association*

REA's HANDBOOK OF ENGLISH
Grammar, Style, and Writing

All the essentials that you need are contained in this simple and practical book

Learn quickly and easily all you need to know about

- Rules and exceptions in grammar
- Spelling and proper punctuation
- Common errors in sentence structure
- Correct usage from 2,000 examples
- Effective writing skills

Complete practice exercises with answers follow each chapter

RĒA RESEARCH & EDUCATION ASSOCIATION

Available at your local bookstore or order directly from us by sending in coupon below.